Pearson Australia
(a division of Pearson Australia Group Pty Ltd)
707 Collins Street, Melbourne, Victoria 3008
PO Box 23360, Melbourne, Victoria 8012
www.pearson.com.au

First published 2017 by Pearson Australia
2023 2022 2021 2020
10 9 8 7 6 5 4 3 2 1

Series Publisher: Tim Carruthers
Content and Learning Specialist: Aynur Bulut
Project Managers: Tamara D'Mello-Pirois, Emma-Jane McCarroll, Jennifer Boyce
Production Managers: Diane Leyman, Shahara Ahmed
Editor: Jane Fitzpatrick
Lead Editor: Daniel Hernández
Designers: Glen McClay, Nikki M Group, Anne Donald
Illustrators: Sunset Publishing Services, diacriTech, Nikki M Group
Typesetters: Nikki M Group
Rights & Permissions Editor: Justin Lim
Series Cover Design: Anne Donald
Cover Image: Shutterstock/Philip Meyer, p. i

Printed and bound in Australia by Pegasus Media & Logistics

978 1 4886 1403 3

Pearson Australia Group Pty Ltd ABN 40 004 245 943

Contents

Introduction

Welcome to the ***Pearson Mathematics 8 Homework Program***.

These homework program worksheets cover systematic and cumulative basic skills revision *and* lesson material from the *Pearson Mathematics 8* Student Book.

The features of the program:

- designed to be used with the *Pearson Mathematics 8* Student Book
- includes 30 double-sided worksheets, covering the entire year
- each worksheet includes a Skills side, which covers basic maths skills, as well as a Practice side, which covers material from the Student Book
- designed for easy correction as a whole class or individually
- results pages are included so students can track their own development.

Full answers for every question are available to teachers from the *Pearson Mathematics 8* eBook or the Pearson Places website.

Pearson Mathematics Homework Program

8

Skills worksheet results

Name: ....

Class: ....

Teacher: ....

Shade or tick the square if you got the answer correct.

Skills question	1A	1B	1C	1D	2A	2B	2C	2D	Skill to learn	Moderate skill shown	Strong skill shown
1 Integers (+, –, ×)											
2 Dividing integers to 12											
3 Multiplying and dividing by multiples of 10											
4 Multiplying and dividing larger numbers											
5 Number patterns											
6 Factors, multiples and primes											
7 Order of operations (including integers)											
8 Fractions (+, –, ×, ÷)											
9 Fractions and decimals (simplifying, comparing, rounding)											
10 Percentages											
11 Decimals (+, –, ×, ÷)											
12 Powers and roots											
13 Algebra — equations and expressions											
14 Algebra — substitution and like terms											
15 Angles, location and geometry											
16 Statistics, probability and graphs											
17 Units, perimeter, area and volume											
Total correct											

ISBN 978 1 4886 1403 3

Pearson Mathematics Homework Program

8

Skills worksheet results

Name: ....

Class: ....

Teacher: ....

Shade or tick the square if you got the answer correct.

Skills question	3A	3B	3C	4A	4B	4C	5A	5B	5C	5D	Skill to learn	Moderate skill shown	Strong skill shown
1 Integers (+, −, ×)													
2 Dividing integers to 12													
3 Multiplying and dividing by multiples of 10													
4 Multiplying and dividing larger numbers													
5 Number patterns													
6 Factors, multiples and primes													
7 Order of operations (including integers)													
8 Fractions (+, −, ×, ÷)													
9 Fractions and decimals (simplifying, comparing, rounding)													
10 Percentages and ratios													
11 Decimals (+, −, ×, ÷)													
12 Powers and roots													
13 Algebra — equations and expressions													
14 Algebra — substitution and like terms													
15 Angles, location and geometry													
16 Statistics, probability and graphs													
17 Units, perimeter, area and volume													
Total correct													

ISBN 978 1 4886 1403 3

Pearson Mathematics Homework Program

8

Skills worksheet results

Name: ....

Class: ....

Teacher: ....

Shade or tick the square if you got the answer correct.

Skills question	6A	6B	6C	7A	7B	7C	Skill to learn	Moderate skill shown	Strong skill shown
1 Integers (+, –, ×)									
2 Dividing integers to 12									
3 Multiplying and dividing by multiples of 10									
4 Multiplying and dividing larger numbers									
5 Number patterns									
6 Factors, multiples and primes									
7 Order of operations (including integers)									
8 Fractions (+, –, ×, ÷)									
9 Fractions and decimals (simplifying, comparing, rounding)									
10 Percentages and ratios									
11 Decimals (+, –, ×, ÷)									
12 Indices and algebraic simplification									
13 Algebra — equations									
14 Algebra — substitution and like terms									
15 Angles, location and geometry									
16 Statistics, probability and graphs									
17 Units, perimeter, area and volume									
Total correct									

Pearson Mathematics Homework Program

8

Skills worksheet results

Name: ....

Class: ....

Teacher: ....

Shade or tick the square if you got the answer correct.

Skills question	8A	8B	8C	9A	9B	9C	Skill to learn	Moderate skill shown	Strong skill shown
1 Integers (+, −, ×)									
2 Dividing integers to 12									
3 Multiplying and dividing by multiples of 10									
4 Multiplying and dividing larger numbers									
5 Number patterns									
6 Factors, multiples and primes									
7 Order of operations (including integers)									
8 Fractions (+, −, ×, ÷)									
9 Fractions and decimals (simplifying, comparing, rounding)									
10 Percentages and ratios									
11 Decimals (+, −, ×, ÷)									
12 Indices and algebraic simplification									
13 Algebra — equations									
14 Algebra — substitution and like terms									
15 Angles, location and geometry									
16 Statistics, probability and graphs									
17 Units, perimeter, area and volume									
Total correct									

ISBN 978 1 4886 1403 3

Pearson Mathematics 8 Homework Program

Integers and indices

Skills 1A

Skills & Practice: Total marks /27

Name: ....

Class: ....

Teacher: ....

This side of this worksheet reviews number skills. The other side of this worksheet refers to *Pearson Mathematics 8* Chapter 1 'Integers and indices' sections 1.1 and 1.2.

1 Complete the table below:

	-9	4	-7	12	-5	11	-3	8	-6
+ 6									

2 Complete the table below:

	132	-44	99	-11	55	-110	33	-88	121
÷ -11									

3 Evaluate 190×1000.

4 Evaluate $256 \div 2$.

5 What are the next three numbers in the sequence?

2, 6, 18, 54, …

6 List all the factors of 32 in ascending order.

7 Evaluate $-5 \times 4 - 7 \times -2$.

8 Evaluate $\frac{3}{4} + \frac{7}{16}$.

9 Write $\frac{87}{12}$ as a mixed number.

10 Find 25% of \$440.

11 Evaluate $45.9 - 37.6$.

12 Evaluate 11^2.

13 Write an equation for this problem.

'A number is divided by 3 and then 4 is added. The result is 10.'

14 If $k = -3$, find the value of $-6k + 5$.

15 Use a protractor to measure this angle.

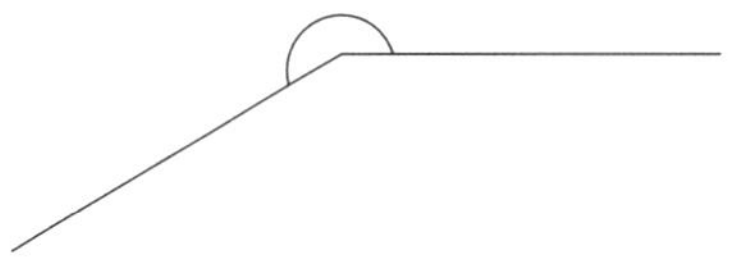

16 A ten-sided die has the numbers 0 to 9 on its faces. What is the probability of rolling an odd number?

17 How many square centimetres are in 1 m^2?

Skills 1A mark: /17

ISBN 978 1 4886 1403 3

Pearson Mathematics 8 Homework Program

Integers and indices

Practice 1A

This side of this worksheet covers *Pearson Mathematics 8* Chapter 1 'Integers and indices' sections 1.1 and 1.2.

For online help, go to your *Pearson Mathematics 8* eBook.

1 Evaluate -3 – (+1).

2 Evaluate 13 + (-5).

3 Evaluate -4 + 6 – 2.

4 Evaluate 12 + (+3) – (-4).

5 Fill in the missing directed numbers so that each row, column and diagonal adds to the same total.

7	-7	-6	4
-4	2	1	
	-2		
			-8

6 Complete each of the following sentences using 'positive' or 'negative'.

A positive multiplied by a negative will give a ______________ answer.

A negative multiplied by a negative will give a ______________ answer.

Multiplying different signs will give a ______________ answer.

Multiplying like signs will give a ______________ answer.

7 Evaluate +2 × -5.

8 Evaluate -2 × -1 × -2.

9 Ethan bought chocolate milk from the school canteen every day for 5 days in a row. Each day he didn't have enough money, so he borrowed $1 from his friend Matt. Write the money Ethan owes Matt as a number sentence using directed numbers, and then find how much money Ethan owes Matt.

10 Evaluate 2 × -5 × 4 × -1.

Practice 1A mark: /10

ISBN 978 1 4886 1403 3

Pearson Mathematics 8 Homework Program

Integers and indices

Skills 1B

Skills & Practice: Total marks /27

Name: ....

Class: ....

Teacher: ....

This side of this worksheet reviews number skills. The other side of this worksheet refers to *Pearson Mathematics 8* Chapter 1 'Integers and indices' sections 1.3 and 1.4.

1 Complete the table below:

	8	-3	12	6	-11	7	-4	-9	5
× -8									

2 Complete the table below:

	-54	36	-99	27	-108	81	72	-45	63
÷ 9									

3 Evaluate 120 × 1000.

4 Evaluate 364 ÷ 7.

5 What are the next three numbers in the sequence?

800, 400, 200, 100, 50, …

6 What is the lowest common multiple of 12 and 15?

7 Evaluate -4 × (2 + -3).

8 Evaluate $1\frac{1}{3} \div \frac{4}{9}$.

9 What is 0.3709 rounded to 2 decimal places?

10 Write 0.25 as a percentage.

11 Evaluate 0.534 + 0.629.

12 Evaluate 2^4.

13 Solve the equation.
$10u = 9$

14 Simplify $10u + 5v + 7u + 2v$.

15 Draw an equilateral triangle.

16 In a box of chocolates there are 12 milk chocolates, 8 white chocolates and 4 dark chocolates. If you randomly take a chocolate, what is the probability that it is a dark chocolate?

17 What is the perimeter of this shape in centimetres?

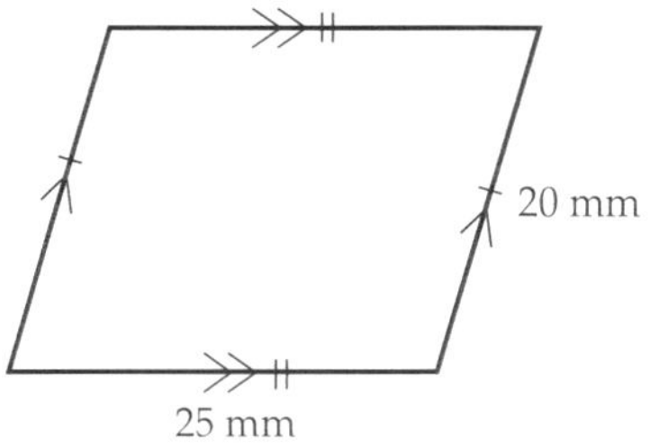

Skills 1B mark: /17

ISBN 978 1 4886 1403 3

Pearson Mathematics Homework Program 8

Integers and indices

Practice 1B

Show all your working

This side of this worksheet covers *Pearson Mathematics 8* Chapter 1 'Integers and indices' sections 1.3 and 1.4.

For online help, go to your *Pearson Mathematics 8* eBook.

1 Calculate:

$-40 \div 5$

2 Calculate:

$-100 \div -10$

3 Calculate:

$24 \div -6$

4 Calculate:

$-48 \div (6 \div -2) - 6$

5 A shop has trouble selling a box of 12 packets of brussels-sprout chips, so it is decided to throw out the box, making a loss of $12. What is the loss per packet?

6 Evaluate:

$5 - 12 + (-2 \times -5)$

7 Evaluate:

$(-2 - 2) \div (-3 + 1)$

8 Evaluate:

$-5 + 3^2 - 1$

9 Evaluate:

$20 \div (3 - 5) \times -1$

10 Over a 6-day period in London, the minimum temperatures are -1 °C, -3 °C, -4 °C, 1 °C, -3 °C, -2 °C. What is the average minimum temperature over those 6 days?

Practice 1B mark: /10

ISBN 978 1 4886 1403 3

Pearson Mathematics 8 Homework Program

Integers and indices

Skills 1C

Skills & Practice: Total marks /27

Name: ....

Class: ....

Teacher: ....

This side of this worksheet reviews number skills. The other side of this worksheet refers to *Pearson Mathematics 8* Chapter 1 'Integers and indices' section 1.5.

1 Complete the table below:

	-3	4	7	-12	8	11	-9	10	-6
× -6									

2 Complete the table below:

	96	36	-108	60	144	-72	48	-84	132
÷ -12									

3 Evaluate $560 \times 10\,000$.

4 Evaluate $546 \div 6$.

5 What are the next three numbers in the sequence?

$\frac{3}{4}, 1\frac{1}{2}, 3, 6, \ldots$

6 List all the prime numbers between 90 and 100.

7 Evaluate $-12 \div (9 \div -3)$.

8 Evaluate $3\frac{1}{4} - 1\frac{3}{4}$.

9 Insert a < or > symbol to make the expression true.

$\frac{5}{3}$ ☐ $1\frac{7}{9}$

10 What is 30 out of 50 as a percentage?

11 Evaluate $6.4 \div 8$.

12 Evaluate $\sqrt{100}$.

13 Solve the equation.

$\frac{x}{2} = 1.5$

14 If $u = 2$, find the value of $1 + 5u$.

15 Find the value of the angle h in the diagram.

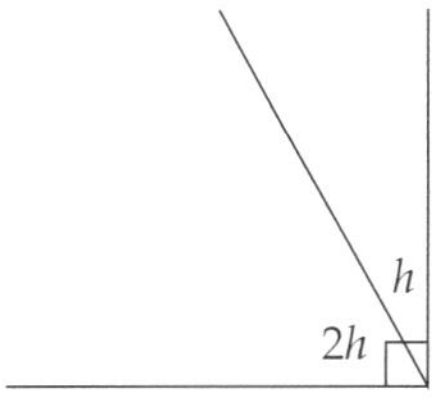

16 Police measured the speeds of 30 vehicles. The results were put into a frequency table.

Speed (km/h)	Frequency
0–40	19
41–50	8
51–60	2
61–100	1
Total	**30**

What percentage of vehicles were travelling at speeds greater than 50 km/h?

17 Find the area of this shape.

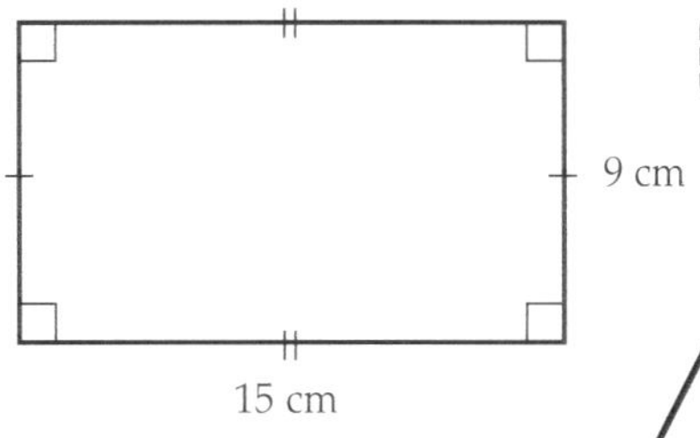

Skills 1C mark: /17

ISBN 978 1 4886 1403 3

Pearson Mathematics 8 Homework Program

Integers and indices

Practice 1C

Show all your working

This side of this worksheet covers *Pearson Mathematics 8* Chapter 1 'Integers and indices' section 1.5.

For online help, go to your *Pearson Mathematics 8* eBook.

1 Write $3 \times 3 \times 3 \times 3 \times 3$ in index form.

2 Write 5^4 in expanded form.

3 Simplify $2^8 \times 2^3$.

4 Simplify $2^5 \div 2^2$ and then evaluate.

5 Simplify $\frac{(-2)^{14}}{(-2)^{12}}$ and then evaluate.

6 Simplify $(5^2 \times 3^4) \div (5^2 \times 3^3)$.

7 Evaluate -2^5.

8 State whether the value of $(-17)^5$ is positive or negative.

9 Simplify $(-3)^4 \times (-3)^5$.

10 Ashley borrows \$1 from a friend. She agrees that the amount she owes will double every day until she pays her friend back. Ashley pays after 5 days. How much did she pay her friend? Give your answer in index form and then evaluate.

Practice 1C mark: /10

ISBN 978 1 4886 1403 3

Pearson Mathematics 8 Homework Program

Integers and indices

Skills 1D

Skills & Practice: Total marks /27

Name:

Class:

Teacher:

This side of this worksheet reviews number skills. The other side of this worksheet refers to *Pearson Mathematics 8* Chapter 1 'Integers and indices' section 1.6.

1 Complete the table below:

	5	-7	11	-6	9	4	10	-8	-12
− 4									

2 Complete the table below:

	-32	80	56	-72	40	-64	96	-48	16
÷ 8									

3 Evaluate 26 700 ÷ 100.

4 Evaluate 298 × 400.

5 What are the next three numbers in the sequence?

3, 8, 15, 24, …

6 Write 60 as a product of its prime factors in index form.

7 Evaluate 14 – -2 × (-7 – -3).

8 Evaluate $1\frac{3}{4} \times 1\frac{1}{7}$.

9 Insert a < or > symbol to make the expression true.

$5\frac{1}{4}$ ☐ $\frac{85}{16}$

10 Write 30% as a fraction in simplest form.

11 Evaluate 1.2 × 6.

12 Write 5 × 5 × 5 × 5 in index form.

13 Simplify $8xy + 4x - 3xy + 5x$.

14 If $g = 3$, what is the value of the expression $3 \times (5 - g) + 1$?

15 How many sides does a hexagon have?

16 This pie graph shows the weekend sports played by a group of 200 Year 8 students at Highview High School. What was the third most popular sport?

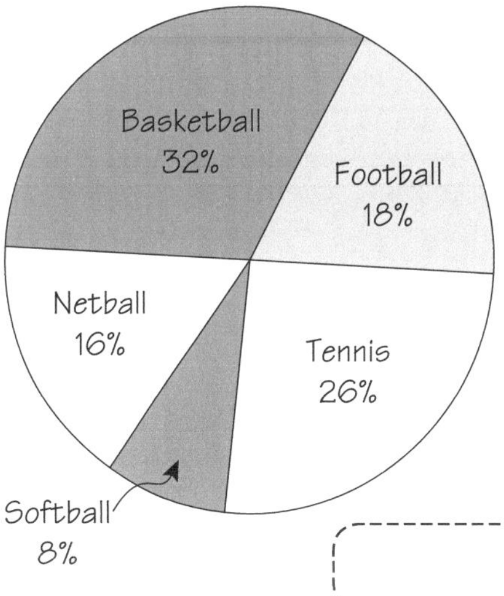

17 Write the area of this triangle as an expression involving x and y.

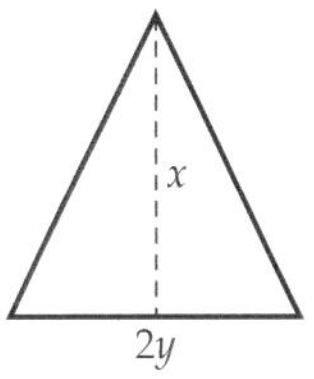

Skills 1D mark: /17

ISBN 978 1 4886 1403 3

Pearson Mathematics 8 Homework Program

Integers and indices

Practice 1D

Show all your working

This side of this worksheet covers *Pearson Mathematics 8* Chapter 1 'Integers and indices' section 1.6.

For online help, go to your *Pearson Mathematics 8* eBook.

1 Write $(2 \times 5)^3$ without brackets.

2 Evaluate $\left(\frac{2}{3}\right)^0$.

3 Simplify $(5^9)^3$.

4 Simplify $(3^4 \times 2^6)^2$.

5 Simplify $\left(\frac{5}{7}\right)^3$.

6 Write 15^4 as a product of two factors raised to a single power.

7 Simplify $\frac{(5 \times 3)^4}{5^2}$.

8 Simplify $(b^4)^3$.

9 Solve for x.

$3^x \times 3^4 = 3^8$

10 Simplify $\frac{3^3 \times 2^2}{(3 \times 2)^0}$.

Practice 1D mark: /10

ISBN 978 1 4886 1403 3

Pearson Mathematics 8 Homework Program

Fractions, decimals and percentages

Skills 2A

Skills & Practice: Total marks /27

Name: ....

Class: ....

Teacher: ....

This side of this worksheet reviews number skills. The other side of this worksheet refers to *Pearson Mathematics 8* Chapter 2 'Fractions, decimals and percentages' sections 2.1, 2.2 and 2.3.

1 Complete the table below:

	-5	10	9	-2	4	11	-6	8	-12
– 10									

2 Complete the table below:

	21	56	84	35	77	49	63	28	42
÷ 7									

3 Evaluate 127×1000.

4 Evaluate 35×9.

5 What are the next three numbers in the sequence?

4, 7, 10, 13, 16, …

6 Is 9 a factor of 504?

7 Evaluate $-7 - 3 \times -2$.

8 Evaluate $1\frac{9}{10} + \frac{3}{10}$.

9 Find which is the bigger fraction:

$\frac{3}{4}$ or $\frac{8}{11}$

10 Find 20% of $350.

11 Evaluate $1.34 + 0.57$.

12 Evaluate 6^2.

13 Write an equation for the following problem.

'A number is doubled and four is added. The result is 10.'

14 If $x = 7$, find the value of $4x + 1$.

15 Use a protractor to measure the angle.

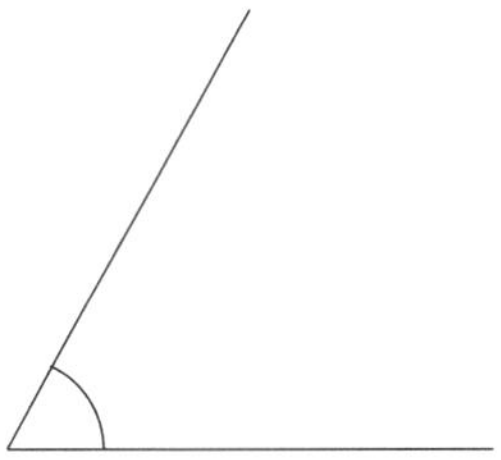

16 The following graph shows the average monthly rainfall (mm) for Wetsville during the first 6 months of the year.

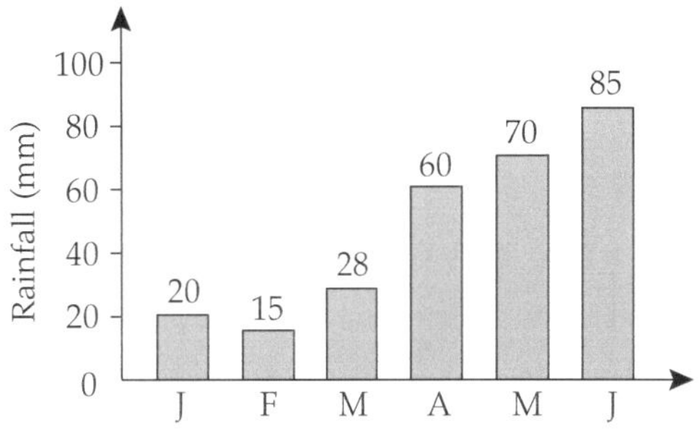

Which is the driest month?

17 How many seconds are in 2.5 hours?

Skills 2A mark: /17

ISBN 978 1 4886 1403 3

Pearson Mathematics Homework Program 8

Fractions, decimals and percentages

Practice 2A

This side of this worksheet covers *Pearson Mathematics 8* Chapter 2 'Fractions, decimals and percentages' sections 2.1, 2.2 and 2.3.

For online help, go to your *Pearson Mathematics 8* eBook.

1 Sort these numbers into ascending order without using a calculator.

$\frac{1}{3}, \frac{1}{4}, 0.3, \frac{2}{5}, 0.6, \frac{5}{9}$

2 Ms Harris had 100 chocolate eggs to share equally among the 28 students of her Year 8 class. How many eggs will each student get and how many will be left over?

3 Write $2\frac{5}{8}$ as a decimal without using a calculator.

4 Write 0.18 as a fraction in simplest form.

5 Is 0.272 727 27… terminating, recurring or irrational?

6 Is $\sqrt{2}$ terminating, recurring or irrational?

7 Write this fraction in exact decimal form.

$\frac{13}{18}$

8 Change this recurring decimal into fraction form.

$0.9\dot{3}$

9 Calculate $-0.7 + 0.3$.

10 Calculate $-\frac{2}{3} \times \frac{1}{4}$.

Practice 2A mark: /10

ISBN 978 1 4886 1403 3

Pearson Mathematics Homework Program 8

Fractions, decimals and percentages

Skills 2B

Skills & Practice: Total marks /27

Name: ....

Class: ....

Teacher: ....

This side of this worksheet reviews number skills. The other side of this worksheet refers to *Pearson Mathematics 8* Chapter 2 'Fractions, decimals and percentages' sections 2.4 and 2.5.

1 Complete the table below:

	2	7	11	4	8	12	3	9	6
$\times 3$									

2 Complete the table below:

	90	30	60	110	10	120	70	40	100
$\div 10$									

3 Evaluate $280 \div 10$.

4 Evaluate 2378×3.

5 What are the next three numbers in the sequence?
26.2, 26.0, 25.8, 25.6, 25.4, …

6 Which of these is not a factor of 16?
1, 2, 4, 16, 32

7 Evaluate $-24 - 3 \times -4$.

8 Evaluate $\frac{4}{5} + \frac{1}{3}$.

9 Which one of these fractions is not equal to $\frac{3}{8}$?

$\frac{6}{16}, \frac{12}{32}, \frac{15}{40}, \frac{26}{72}$

10 Find 25% of 300 kg.

11 Evaluate $2.57 - 1.62$.

12 Evaluate 8^2.

13 Write an equation for the following problem.
'A number is multiplied by 3 and then 6 is subtracted. The result is 9.'

14 If $v = 7$, find the value of $6v + 3$.

15 Use a protractor to measure the angle.

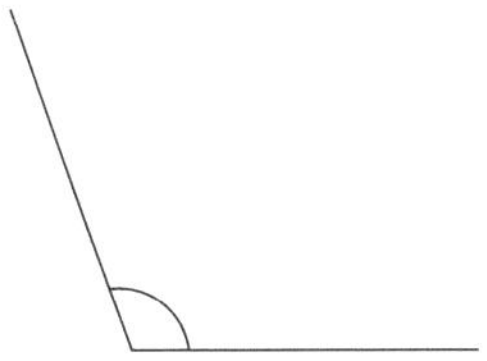

16 A class was surveyed on their favourite type of sport. The results were put into a frequency table. What was the third most popular sport?

Sport	Frequency
Netball	4
Soccer	7
AFL	8
Basketball	6
Other	1
Total	**26**

17 How many metres are in 0.75 km?

Skills 2B mark: /17

ISBN 978 1 4886 1403 3

Pearson Mathematics Homework Program 8

Fractions, decimals and percentages

Practice 2B

Show all your working

This side of this worksheet covers *Pearson Mathematics 8* Chapter 2 'Fractions, decimals and percentages' sections 2.4 and 2.5.

For online help, go to your *Pearson Mathematics 8* eBook.

1 Estimate the percentage of water left in this glass.

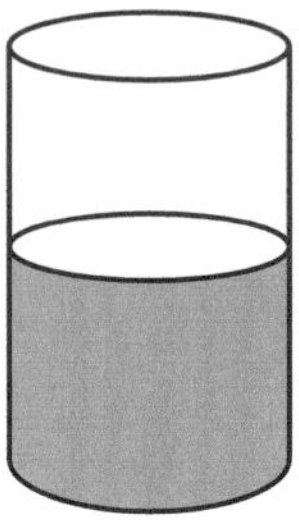

2 Estimate (to the nearest 10%) the percentage of this rectangle that is shaded.

3 Estimate the percentage of the circle that is shaded.

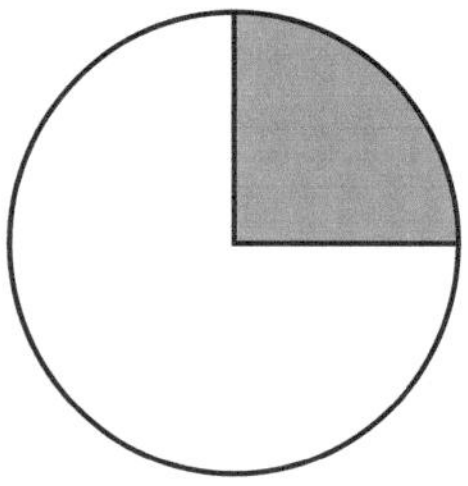

4 Draw a square and shade approximately 30% of it.

5 Write $\frac{1}{4}$ as a percentage.

6 Write 0.85 as a percentage.

7 Write $\frac{3}{8}$ as a percentage.

8 Write 0.362 as a percentage.

9 Write $1\frac{1}{4}$ as a percentage.

10 In Jarrod's family, $\frac{3}{5}$ of the family members are male.

What is this as a percentage?

Practice 2B mark: /10

ISBN 978 1 4886 1403 3

Pearson Mathematics 8 Homework Program

Fractions, decimals and percentages

Skills 2C

Skills & Practice: Total marks /27

Name: ....

Class: ....

Teacher: ....

This side of this worksheet reviews number skills. The other side of this worksheet refers to *Pearson Mathematics 8* Chapter 2 'Fractions, decimals and percentages' sections 2.6 and 2.7.

1 Complete the table below:

	6	-12	3	9	-4	7	-2	8	-5
× -4									

2 Complete the table below:

	-66	36	-12	48	-72	24	-54	42	-30
÷ 6									

3 Evaluate $800 \div 100$.

4 Evaluate 789×9.

5 What are the next three numbers in the sequence?

$1\frac{1}{4}, 1\frac{3}{8}, 1\frac{1}{2}, 1\frac{5}{8}, 1\frac{3}{4}, \ldots$

6 What is the lowest common multiple of 6 and 8?

7 Evaluate $-5 \times 6 \div -10$.

8 Evaluate $1\frac{1}{8} \times \frac{4}{9}$.

9 What is 5.402 rounded to 2 decimal places?

10 What is 20% of a class of 30 students?

11 Evaluate $23.5 + 32.6$.

12 Evaluate 3^3.

13 Solve this equation.

$\frac{x}{3} = 6$

14 Simplify $7h + 4 - 3h + 2$.

15 Is this triangle an acute-angled triangle, an obtuse-angled triangle or a right-angled triangle?

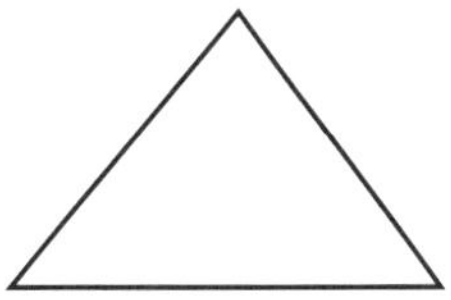

16 Evan tries to play a trick on Rich by weighting a coin so that the probability of getting 'heads' is now 0.4. What is the probability of getting 'tails' on this coin?

17 Find the perimeter of this shape.

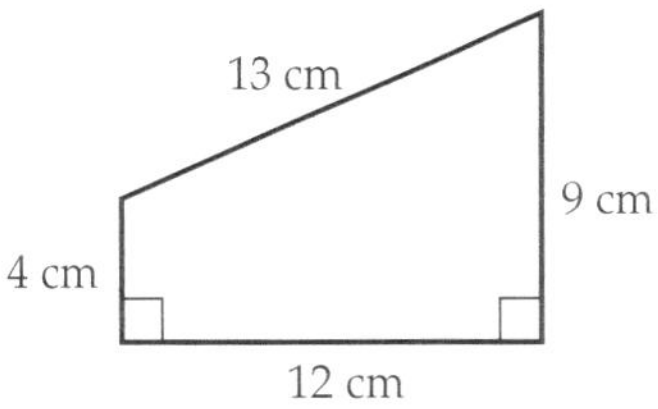

Skills 2C mark: /17

ISBN 978 1 4886 1403 3

Pearson Mathematics 8 Homework Program

Fractions, decimals and percentages

Practice 2C

This side of this worksheet covers *Pearson Mathematics 8* Chapter 2 'Fractions, decimals and percentages' sections 2.6 and 2.7.

For online help, go to your *Pearson Mathematics 8* eBook.

1 Convert 75% to a fraction in simplest form.

2 Convert 87.5% to a fraction in simplest form.

3 Convert 27% to a decimal.

4 Convert $\frac{1}{4}\%$ to a decimal.

5 Kayla had a $6\frac{1}{2}\%$ raise in her salary. By what fraction did her salary increase?

6 Write 24 as a percentage of 25.

7 Write 5 mm as a percentage of 4 cm.

8 Write 4 days as a percentage of 4 weeks (to 2 decimal places).

9 Sarah and Riley are in different classes but both took the same Maths test, which was out of 30 marks. Sarah got 27 marks. Riley got 23 marks, but because his class had less time they didn't do the last question, which was worth five marks. What percentage did each get on the test, and who got the better mark?

10 Jackson gets $20 to spend at the school canteen each week. One week he spends $6 of this on drinks. What percentage of his canteen spending money did Jackson spend on drinks?

Practice 2C mark: /10

ISBN 978 1 4886 1403 3

Pearson Mathematics 8 Homework Program

Fractions, decimals and percentages

Skills 2D

Skills & Practice: Total marks /27

Name:

Class:

Teacher:

This side of this worksheet reviews number skills. The other side of this worksheet refers to *Pearson Mathematics 8* Chapter 2 'Fractions, decimals and percentages' sections 2.8, 2.9 and 2.10.

1 Complete the table below:

	-7	2	-11	4	-8	12	-3	9	-6
− 12									

2 Complete the table below:

	32	96	-16	56	72	-48	64	88	-24
÷ 8									

3 Evaluate 42 000 ÷ 100.

4 Evaluate 3177×8.

5 What are the next three numbers in the sequence?

13.5, 12.6, 11.7, 10.8, …

6 What is the next prime number after 54?

7 Evaluate 5 − (-12) − 7.

8 Evaluate $2\frac{1}{4} - 1\frac{1}{2}$.

9 Insert a < or > symbol to make the expression true.

$1\frac{5}{6}$ ☐ $\frac{5}{3}$

10 What is 30 out of 40 as a percentage?

11 Evaluate 3×0.8.

12 Evaluate $\sqrt{144}$.

13 Solve the equation.
$b - 5 = 12$

14 If w = -1, find the value of $7w + 1$.

15 Find the value of the angle g in the diagram.

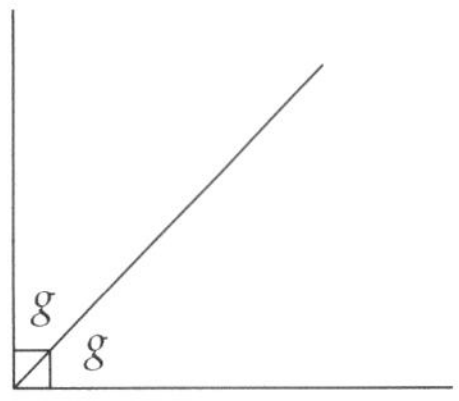

16 Decide whether you would describe the event 'There will be an earthquake at my school tomorrow' as 'impossible', 'not likely', 'likely' or 'certain'.

17 Find the area of the shape.

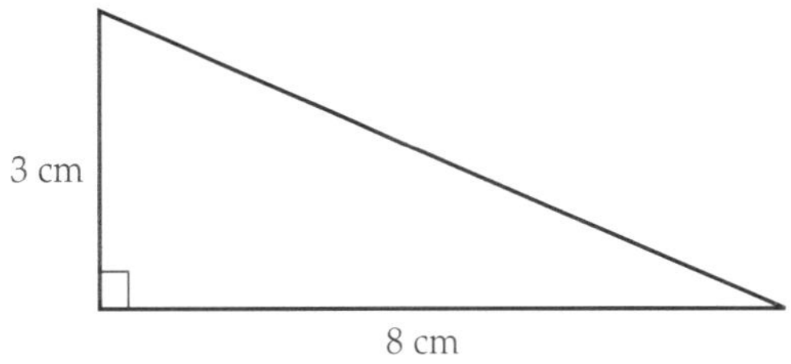

Skills 2D mark: /17

ISBN 978 1 4886 1403 3

Pearson Mathematics 8 Homework Program

Fractions, decimals and percentages

Practice 2D

Show all your working

This side of this worksheet covers *Pearson Mathematics 8* Chapter 2 'Fractions, decimals and percentages' sections 2.8, 2.9 and 2.10.

For online help, go to your *Pearson Mathematics 8* eBook.

1 Find 60% of 200 kg.

2 Is 20% of 5% of 100 the same as 5% of 20% of 100? Explain.

3 A particular bank will only let a person spend a maximum of 40% of their wage repaying the loan on their house. What is the maximum amount that a person earning $1200 a week can repay?

4 In a class of 25 students, 40% of students have brown hair. How many students have brown hair in the class?

5 At Parkhill High there are 200 students in Year 8 and 60% of these students sign up to play football. Of these, 25% get into the interschool team. How many students play in the interschool team?

6 Matthew can run 100 m in 11.80 seconds. He hopes to decrease this time by 10% after more training. What time is he aiming for?

7 Georgia buys a car part that costs $80 plus GST (10%). How much did the part cost?

8 A store offers a 15% discount on everything, so Dan buys a new quilt cover, which originally was $70. What is the sale price of the quilt cover?

9 A clothing store buys jeans for $15 from the wholesaler. If the store's mark-up is 200%, what is the selling price of the jeans?

10 Ella works for a furniture store and earns $900 a week plus a commission of 1% on whatever she sells. What will Ella's weekly earnings be, if she sells $52 000 of furniture in one week?

Practice 2D mark: /10

ISBN 978 1 4886 1403 3

Pearson Mathematics 8 Homework Program

Algebra

Skills 3A

Skills & Practice: Total marks /27

Name: ....

Class: ....

Teacher: ....

This side of this worksheet reviews number skills. The other side of this worksheet refers to *Pearson Mathematics 8* Chapter 3 'Algebra' sections 3.1, 3.2 and 3.3.

1 Complete the table below:

	7	-2	5	-9	6	12	-3	-8	4
− 9									

2 Complete the table below:

	-12	36	24	-72	66	-18	60	-120	6
÷ 6									

3 Evaluate 250 000 ÷ 100.

4 Evaluate 673×2.

5 What are the next three numbers in the sequence?

1024, 256, 64, 16, …

6 List all the factors of 64 in descending order.

7 Evaluate $28 \div (-3 + -4)$.

8 Evaluate $\frac{7}{12} + \frac{5}{18}$.

9 Simplify $\frac{68}{16}$ and write as a mixed number.

10 Find 50% of 56 kg.

11 Evaluate 32.3 – 23.7.

12 Evaluate 30^2.

13 Solve the equation.

$s + 6 = 9$

14 If $x = -4$, find the value of $1 - 5x$.

15 Use a protractor to measure the angle.

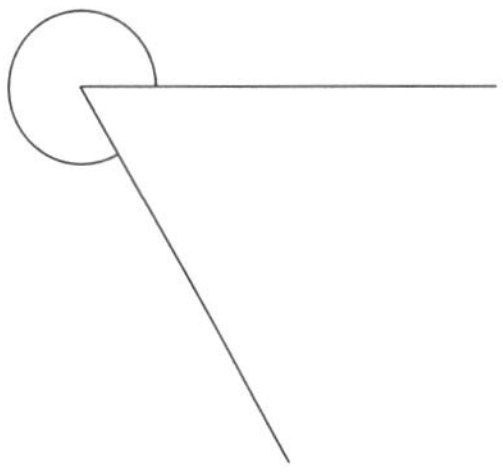

16 Decide whether you would describe the event 'I will eat some food tomorrow' as 'impossible', 'not likely', 'likely' or 'certain'.

17 How many grams are in 2.6 kilograms?

Skills 3A mark: /17

ISBN 978 1 4886 1403 3

Pearson Mathematics 8 Homework Program

Algebra

Practice 3A

This side of this worksheet covers *Pearson Mathematics 8* Chapter 3 'Algebra' sections 3.1, 3.2 and 3.3.

For online help, go to your *Pearson Mathematics 8* eBook.

1 For $-7c + 6d - 3ab + 6 = 2c + b$:

a identify whether it is an expression or equation

b write the coefficient of ab

c write all the terms

d list the variables

e write any constants.

2 Rewrite the following using algebraic conventions.

a $w \times 2 \div 7$

b $k \times d \times -2 \times d$

3 Riley has t markers in his pencil case. Luke originally had double the number Riley did, but he lost four of them. Write an expression for the number of markers that Luke has now.

4 Substitute $x = -4$ and $y = 6$ to find the value of the expression.

$\frac{5x}{4} + \frac{7y}{2}$

5 Use the rule $y = \frac{x}{5} + 1$ to complete the table.

x	5	10	15	30	60
y					

6 Substitute $a = -2$ and $b = -1$ to find the value of the expression.

$2b^2 - a^2$

7 Substitute $a = -1$, $b = 2$ and $c = 5$ into $4a - 7b + 2c$ and evaluate.

8 The formula $a = \frac{v - u}{t}$ gives acceleration. What is the acceleration if $v = 80$, $u = 0$ and $t = 20$?

9 The formula $c = \sqrt{a^2 + b^2}$ gives a right-angled triangle's longest side length, c, from the two shorter side lengths a and b. Find the length of the longest side if $a = 4$ and $b = 3$.

10 The formula $V = \frac{4 \times 3.14 \times r^3}{3}$ gives the approximate volume of a sphere that has radius r. Calculate V if $r = 3$.

Practice 3A mark: /10

ISBN 978 1 4886 1403 3

Pearson Mathematics 8 Homework Program

Algebra

Skills 3B

Skills & Practice: Total marks /27

Name: ....

Class: ....

Teacher: ....

This side of this worksheet reviews number skills. The other side of this worksheet refers to *Pearson Mathematics 8* Chapter 3 'Algebra' sections 3.4 and 3.5.

1 Complete the table below:

	3	-4	7	12	-8	11	-9	10	-6
× 5									

2 Complete the table below:

	33	-44	88	132	-55	121	-11	-110	66
÷ -11									

3 Evaluate 800 ÷ 100.

4 Evaluate 125 × 26.

5 What are the next three numbers in the sequence?

486, 162, 54, 18, …

6 What is the lowest common multiple of 12 and 18?

7 Evaluate (5 + 9) ÷ 7.

8 Evaluate $\frac{8}{9} \times \frac{3}{16}$.

9 What is 0.005 35 rounded to 3 decimal places?

10 What is 0.92 as a percentage?

11 Evaluate 17.95 + 19.95.

12 Evaluate 1^4.

13 Solve the equation.

$12w = 6$

14 Simplify $7 + 7i + 4k - 3 + 2k + 2i$.

15 What is this type of shape called?

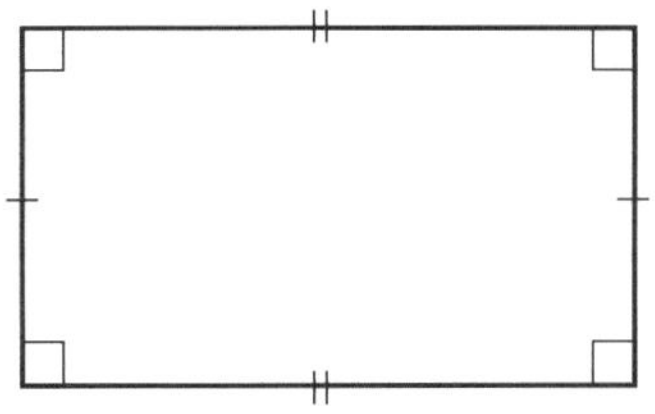

16 A ten-sided die has the numbers 0 to 9 on its faces. What is the probability of rolling a number that is divisible by 9?

17 Write the perimeter of this shape as an expression involving x.

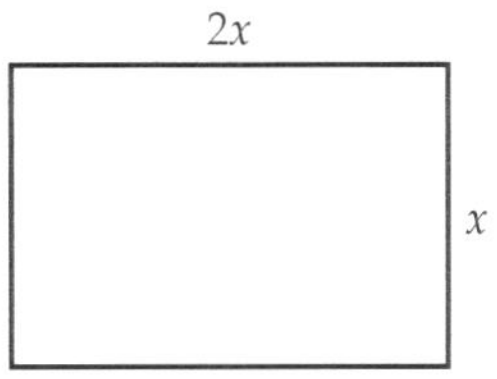

Skills 3B mark: /17

ISBN 978 1 4886 1403 3

Pearson Mathematics 8 Homework Program

Algebra

Practice 3B

Show all your working

This side of this worksheet covers *Pearson Mathematics 8* Chapter 3 'Algebra' sections 3.4 and 3.5.

For online help, go to your *Pearson Mathematics 8* eBook.

1 Underline all terms that are like terms to $3cd$.

$3c$, cd, $5d$, $-5cd$, $2cd^2$, $3dc$

2 Simplify $10a - 9a$.

3 Simplify $7h + 4k - 3h + 2k$.

4 Simplify $12 + 4x + 5y + 2xy - 2x + xy - 10 + 2y$.

5 In Tran's wallet there are two types of coins: silver and gold. He has five silver coins and four gold coins. Kelly has eight silver coins and two gold coins. They put their coins together to buy lunch. If s is the value of the silver coin and g is the value of the gold coin, write an expression for the total value of the coins.

6 Simplify $4 \times 3e$.

7 Simplify $4e \div 2e$.

8 Simplify $\frac{24g}{8}$.

9 Simplify $-2 \times 2f \times 3g$.

10 Simplify $\frac{12mn}{3n}$.

Practice 3B mark: /10

ISBN 978 1 4886 1403 3

Pearson Mathematics 8 Homework Program

Algebra

Skills 3C

Skills & Practice: Total marks /27

Name:

Class:

Teacher:

This side of this worksheet reviews number skills. The other side of this worksheet refers to *Pearson Mathematics 8* Chapter 3 'Algebra' sections 3.6 and 3.7.

1 Complete the table below:

	3	-4	7	-12	8	11	-9	-10	6
$\times 2$									

2 Complete the table below:

	-72	132	-96	60	144	-48	108	-36	84
$\div -12$									

3 Evaluate 43 000 ÷ 1000.

4 Evaluate 567×35.

5 What are the next three numbers in the sequence?
210 000, 21 000, 2100, 210, …

6 List all the prime factors of 42.

7 Evaluate $-24 \times (7 + -5)$.

8 Evaluate $3\frac{1}{5} - 1\frac{3}{5}$.

9 Insert a < or > symbol to make the expression true.

$1\frac{5}{16} \ \square \ \frac{7}{4}$

10 What is 18 out of 20 as a percentage?

11 Evaluate 0.5×0.9.

12 Evaluate $\sqrt{400}$.

13 Solve this equation.

$2x + 1 = 5$

14 If $a = 7$ and $b = 2$, find the value of ab.

15 Find the value of the angle p in the diagram.

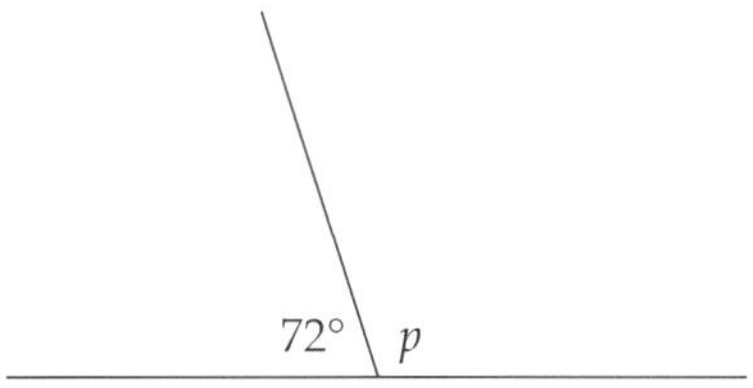

16 What is the probability of rolling a factor of 6 on a standard six-sided die?

17 Find the area of the shaded shape.

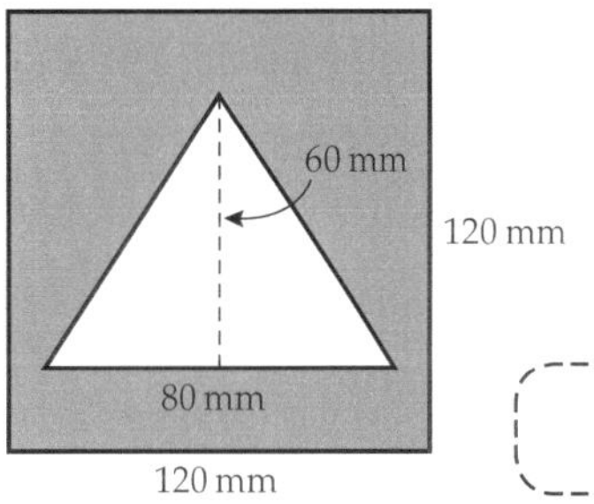

Skills 3C mark: /17

ISBN 978 1 4886 1403 3

Pearson Mathematics Homework Program 8

Algebra

Practice 3C

Show all your working

This side of this worksheet covers *Pearson Mathematics 8* Chapter 3 'Algebra' sections 3.6 and 3.7.

For online help, go to your *Pearson Mathematics 8* eBook.

1 Expand $5(b - 6)$.

2 Expand $3(5a - 4)$.

3 Expand $2f(3de + d^2)$.

4 Expand $2b(4c - 7) + 3c(b + 3) + 10b$ and simplify by collecting like terms.

5 A rectangle has a width of $2x$ metres and a length of $(y - 3)$ metres. Write an expression for the area of the rectangle and expand the brackets.

6 Find the highest common factor of these terms.

$12r^3s^4$ and $18r^2s^5$

7 Factorise this expression by taking out the highest common factor.

$6e - 14$

8 Factorise this expression by taking out the highest common factor.

$xy + 4x$

9 Factorise this expression by taking out the highest common factor.

$15e - 25ef$

10 Factorise this expression by taking out the highest common factor.

$2(x + 1) + y(x + 1)$

Practice 3C mark: /10

  ISBN 978 1 4886 1403 3

Pearson Mathematics 8 Homework Program

Ratio and rate

Skills 4A

Skills & Practice: Total marks /27

Name:

Class:

Teacher:

This side of this worksheet reviews number skills. The other side of this worksheet refers to *Pearson Mathematics 8* Chapter 4 'Ratio and rate' sections 4.1, 4.2 and 4.3.

1 Complete the table below:

	-11	2	-7	4	8	-5	9	-6	12
− 11									

2 Complete the table below:

	-120	22	12	-4	6	-200	20	-16	64
÷ 2									

3 Evaluate 29.8×1000.

4 Evaluate $1285 \div 5$.

5 What are the next three numbers in the sequence?
12.4, 12.43, 12.46, 12.49, …

6 Is 9 a factor of 3026?

7 Evaluate $3 - 2 \times 6 \div -4$.

8 Evaluate $\frac{5}{12} + \frac{5}{6}$.

9 Simplify $\frac{80}{24}$ and write as a mixed number.

10 Find 60% of $2000.

11 Evaluate $2.345 - 1.567$.

12 Evaluate 70^2.

13 Solve this equation.
$4x + 5 = 13$

14 If $a = 6$ and $b = 12$, find the value of $\frac{b}{a}$.

15 How many faces does a tetrahedron have?

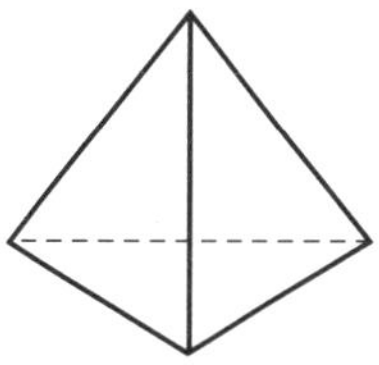

16 Hannah's marks for her last three Maths homework sheets were 26, 27 and 25. What is her average mark?

17 How many litres are in 56 000 mL?

Skills 4A mark: /17

ISBN 978 1 4886 1403 3

Pearson Mathematics Homework Program 8

Ratio and rate

Practice 4A

Show all your working

This side of this worksheet covers *Pearson Mathematics 8* Chapter 4 'Ratio and rate' sections 4.1, 4.2 and 4.3.

For online help, go to your *Pearson Mathematics 8* eBook.

1 A class has 18 students with pets and 12 students without pets. Write this as a ratio of students without pets to students with pets.

2 Refer to the previous question. Write the ratio of students without pets to the total number of students in the class.

3 Refer to the previous question. What fraction of the class have pets?

4 Write this ratio in simplest form.

16:24

5 Write this ratio in simplest form.

\$6:50c

6 Write this ratio in simplest form.

$30\text{ min}:2\text{ h}:1\frac{1}{2}\text{ h}$

7 Harrison travels 3.5 km to get to school and Haley travels 700 m. Find the ratio of distance travelled by Harrison to distance travelled by Haley in simplest form.

8 Write the following as a unit ratio.

11.64:9.7

9 Cindy is 1.80 m tall and her son is 72 cm tall. How many times taller is Cindy than her son?

10 Refer to the previous question. If the scale factor between the heights of Cindy and her son eight years later is 1.2, how much has her son grown? (Assume that Cindy hasn't grown.)

Practice 4A mark: /10

  ISBN 978 1 4886 1403 3

Pearson Mathematics Homework Program 8

Ratio and rate

Skills 4B

Skills & Practice: Total marks /27

Name: ....

Class: ....

Teacher: ....

This side of this worksheet reviews number skills. The other side of this worksheet refers to *Pearson Mathematics 8* Chapter 4 'Ratio and rate' sections 4.4 and 4.5.

1 Complete the table below:

	6	-9	4	-7	-12	2	-11	5	-8
+ 12									

2 Complete the table below:

	21	-9	24	-18	33	-15	36	-27	6
÷ -3									

3 Evaluate 60×100.

4 Evaluate $8604 \div 9$.

5 What are the next three numbers in the sequence?

3, 12, 48, 192, …

6 What is the lowest common multiple of 24 and 72?

7 Evaluate $17 - 6 \times 2 - -5$.

8 Evaluate $\frac{7}{12} \div \frac{21}{32}$.

9 What is 2.172 rounded to 1 decimal place?

10 Write 0.4 as a percentage.

11 Evaluate $14.50 + 49.95$.

12 Evaluate 2^5.

13 Solve this equation.

$\frac{x}{2} + 3 = 8$

14 Simplify $0.7k + 2.1m - 0.3k + 1.3m$.

15 What are the coordinates of the point below?

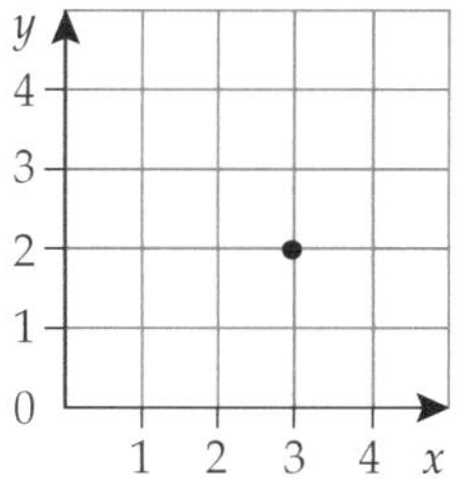

16 A class was surveyed on what pets they each owned. The results were put into a frequency table. What was the least popular pet?

Pet	Frequency
Dog	15
Cat	9
Rat	2
Bird	1
Total	**27**

17 What is the side length of a square tile that has a perimeter of 56 cm?

Skills 4B mark: /17

ISBN 978 1 4886 1403 3

Pearson Mathematics 8 Homework Program

Ratio and rate

Practice 4B

Show all your working

This side of this worksheet covers *Pearson Mathematics 8* Chapter 4 'Ratio and rate' sections 4.4 and 4.5.

For online help, go to your *Pearson Mathematics 8* eBook.

1 Find the value of n.

$2:5 = 6:n$

2 Find the value of n.

$3:n = 6:5$

3 Find the value of n.

$5:n = 6:3$

4 On a school excursion, the adult to student ratio needs to be 1:5. If 45 students are going on the excursion, how many adults are needed?

5 The ratio of the width of a painting to its length is 3:5. If the length is 250 cm, what is the width?

6 Convert 4 mm:20 cm to a scale ratio and underline the scale factor.

7 A town plan is drawn to a scale of 1:2000. If a building is 3 cm wide on the plan, what is its real width?

8 Is 3:8100 a unit ratio?

9 The length of a bedroom is 3 m. What is its diagram length if the scale is 1:20?

10 A 10 km road is 2 cm long on a map. What is the scale ratio?

Practice 4B mark: /10

  ISBN 978 1 4886 1403 3

Pearson Mathematics 8 Homework Program

Ratio and rate

Skills 4C

Skills & Practice: Total marks /27

Name: ....

Class: ....

Teacher: ....

This side of this worksheet reviews number skills. The other side of this worksheet refers to *Pearson Mathematics 8* Chapter 4 'Ratio and rate' sections 4.6 and 4.7.

1 Complete the table below:

	9	-5	7	-2	12	-4	8	3	-6
× -3									

2 Complete the table below:

	-36	90	-72	108	81	-54	18	-45	27
÷ 9									

3 Evaluate 352×1000.

4 Evaluate $3076 \div 4$.

5 What are the next three numbers in the sequence?

$10\frac{1}{3}, 9\frac{2}{3}, 9, 8\frac{1}{3}, \ldots$

6 Write 36 as a product of its prime factors in index form.

7 Evaluate $-3 \times -6 \div 9 \times -4$.

8 Evaluate $5\frac{2}{7} - \frac{5}{14}$.

9 Insert a < or > symbol to make the expression true.

$\frac{17}{5}$ ☐ $3\frac{4}{15}$

10 What is 22 out of 25 as a percentage?

11 Evaluate $0.72 \div 9$.

12 Evaluate $\sqrt{2500}$.

13 Solve this equation.

$2(x - 1) = 8$

14 If $j = 0.1$ and $k = 0.3$, find the value of $2jk$.

15 Find the value of the angle m in the diagram.

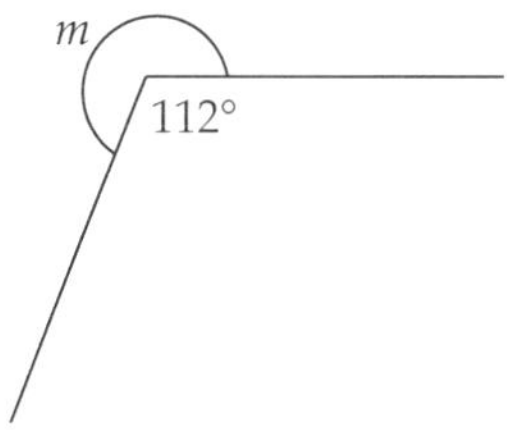

16 What is the probability of spinning the spinner shown and getting a prime number?

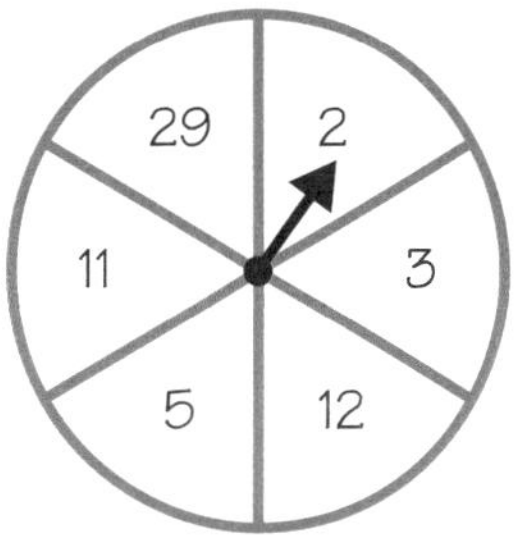

17 What is the area of this shape?

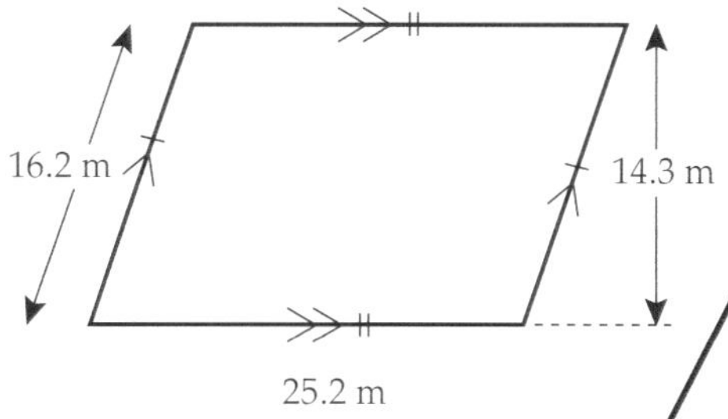

Skills 4C mark: /17

Pearson Mathematics 8 Homework Program

Ratio and rate

Practice 4C

Show all your working

This side of this worksheet covers *Pearson Mathematics 8* Chapter 4 'Ratio and rate' sections 4.6 and 4.7.

For online help, go to your *Pearson Mathematics 8* eBook.

1 How many parts are in the ratio 4:3:5?

2 Divide $60 in the ratio 2:3.

3 Cordial is made by mixing a concentrate with water in the ratio of 1:4. How much concentrate and water is needed to make up 2 L of cordial?

4 The ratio of Year 7, Year 8 and Year 9 students at Pythagoras High is 3:4:3. If there are 500 students in total in Years 7, 8 and 9, then how many students are in Year 8?

5 The win:loss:draw ratio of a soccer team is 2:3:1. How many games has the team won if they have played 12 games?

6 What is the cost of petrol, in cents per litre, if 40 litres costs $57.20?

7 The Adams family took 6 hours to drive 300 km. What was their average speed?

8 How much time would it take to travel 560 km, if your average speed is 70 km/h?

9 Charles sends an average of 9 chat messages per day. What is the average number of messages he would send in one week?

10 A car travelled at 90 km/h for 5 minutes, at 60 km/h for 10 minutes and at 70 km/h for 15 minutes. How far did the car travel in total?

Practice 4C mark: /10

ISBN 978 1 4886 1403 3

Pearson Mathematics 8 Homework Program

Measurement

Skills 5A

Skills & Practice: Total marks /27

Name:

Class:

Teacher:

This side of this worksheet reviews number skills. The other side of this worksheet refers to *Pearson Mathematics 8* Chapter 5 'Measurement' sections 5.1, 5.2 and 5.3.

1 Complete the table below:

	6	-12	7	3	-8	-4	9	-5	11
× 2									

2 Complete the table below:

	-72	42	-30	54	48	-12	18	-66	36
÷ -6									

3 Evaluate 1230 ÷ 100.

4 Evaluate 246 × 20.

5 What are the next three numbers in the sequence?

2, 3, 5, 8, 12, …

6 List all the common factors of 20 and 50.

7 Evaluate -6 × 7 – 24 ÷ -4.

8 Evaluate $1\frac{3}{8} + \frac{5}{6}$.

9 Simplify $\frac{117}{36}$ and write as a mixed number.

10 Find 12% of 400 minutes.

11 Evaluate 134.7 – 125.2.

12 Write 4 × 4 × 4 in index form.

13 Solve this equation.

$9x - 5 = 13$

14 If $x = 3$, find the value of $4x^2$.

15 How many edges does a cube have?

16 There are 5 pens, 3 pencils and 2 highlighters in Nick's pencil case. What is the largest number of writing tools that Nick could take from the case before he gets a pencil?

17 How many cubic centimetres are in 1 m^3?

Skills 5A mark: /17

ISBN 978 1 4886 1403 3

Pearson Mathematics Homework Program 8

Measurement

Practice 5A

Show all your working

This side of this worksheet covers *Pearson Mathematics 8* Chapter 5 'Measurement' sections 5.1, 5.2 and 5.3.

For online help, go to your *Pearson Mathematics 8* eBook.

1 Find the perimeter of this shape.

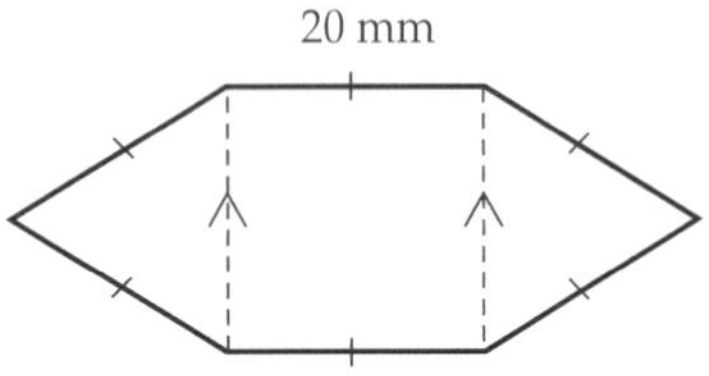

2 Find the perimeter of this shape. All measurements are in metres.

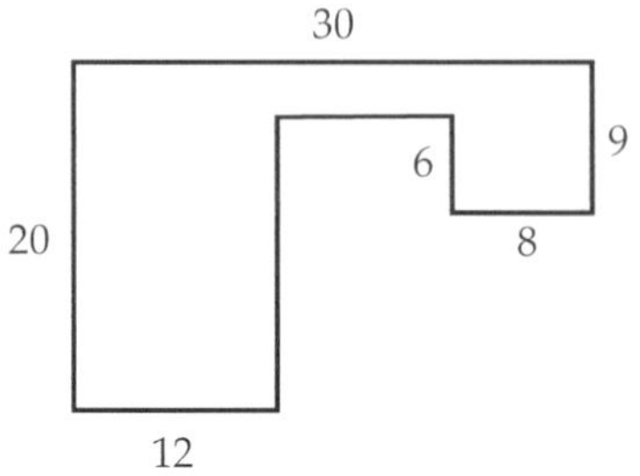

3 If a square has a perimeter of 6 cm, what is the length of one of its sides?

4 A rectangular yard with dimensions 10 m by 12 m needs to be fenced. The fence is made of metal posts with 3 rows of wire. How many metres of wire will be needed?

5 Hayley has just enough string to make a rectangle that has a length of 14 cm and a width of 8 cm. What is the side length of the square she could make with the same piece of string?

6 What is the value of a circle's $\frac{\text{circumference}}{\text{diameter}}$ to 3 decimal places?

7 Calculate the circumference of this circle correct to 2 decimal places.

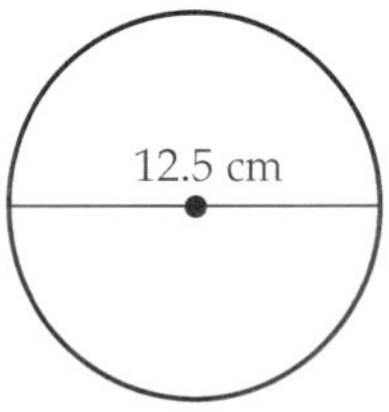

8 Calculate the circumference of this circle correct to 2 decimal places.

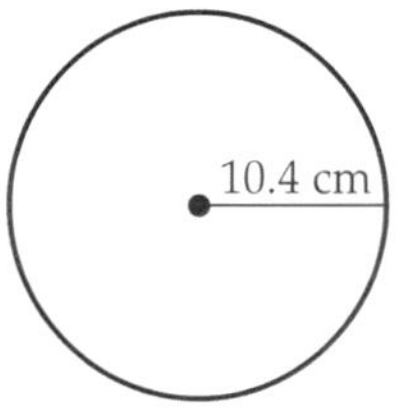

9 Calculate the perimeter of this semicircle correct to 2 decimal places.

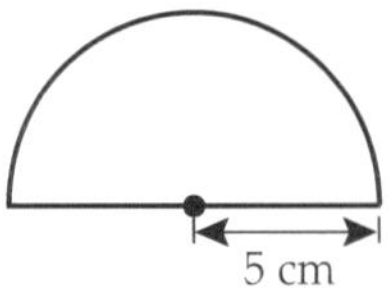

10 Calculate the circumference of this circle correct to 1 decimal place.

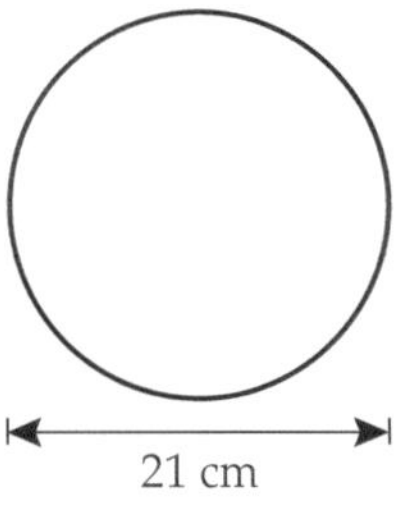

Practice 5A mark: /10

  ISBN 978 1 4886 1403 3

Pearson Mathematics 8 Homework Program

Measurement

Skills 5B

Skills & Practice: Total marks /27

Name:

Class:

Teacher:

This side of this worksheet reviews number skills. The other side of this worksheet refers to *Pearson Mathematics 8* Chapter 5 'Measurement' sections 5.4 and 5.5.

1 Complete the table below:

	-5	-8	-12	6	-9	3	-11	7	-4
+ 6									

2 Complete the table below:

	12	-40	28	-80	48	-120	16	-24	32
÷ 4									

3 Evaluate $9800 \div 1000$.

4 Evaluate 876×70.

5 What are the next three numbers in the sequence?

12, 21, 29, 36, 42, …

6 Which of the following are multiples of 9?

3, 27, 1, 99, 9

7 Evaluate $-27 - 3 \times -4 - 24 \div -8$.

8 Evaluate $2\frac{1}{4} \div \frac{4}{9}$.

9 What is 0.317 82 rounded to 3 decimal places?

10 Write 0.02 as a percentage.

11 Evaluate $2.347 + 5.782$.

12 Write 2^3 in expanded form.

13 Solve this equation.

$4(x + 3) = 20$

14 Simplify $h^2 + 4h - 3h + 2h^2$.

15 What are the coordinates of the point below?

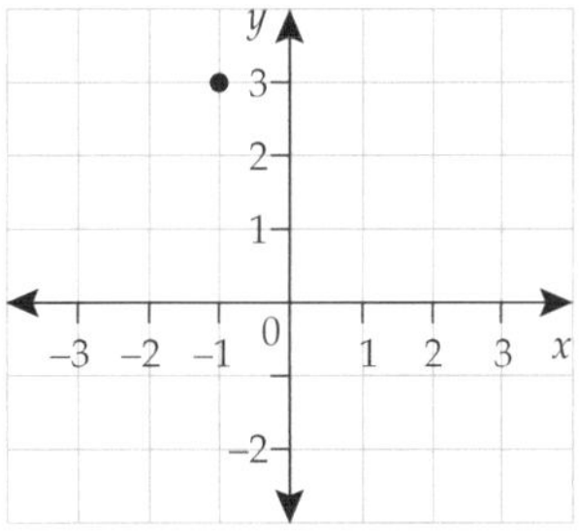

16 A class was surveyed on how much time they spent using a computer the night before, to the nearest hour. What was the most common number of hours of computer usage?

Hours of computer use	Frequency
0	4
1	8
2	9
3 or more	3
Total	**24**

17 What is the perimeter of this shape?

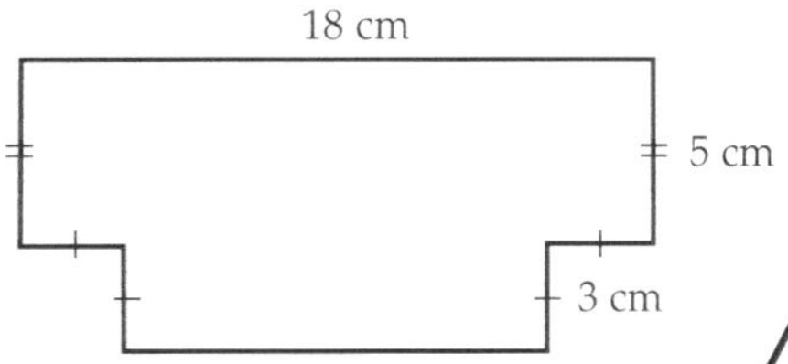

Skills 5B mark: /17

ISBN 978 1 4886 1403 3

Pearson Mathematics 8 Homework Program

Measurement

Practice 5B

Show all your working

This side of this worksheet covers *Pearson Mathematics 8* Chapter 5 'Measurement' sections 5.4 and 5.5.

For online help, go to your *Pearson Mathematics 8* eBook.

1 Complete the conversion.

$4.7 \text{ m}^2 =$ ____________________ mm^2

2 Find the area of a rectangle that has a width of 7 cm and length of 12 cm.

3 Find the area of this triangle.

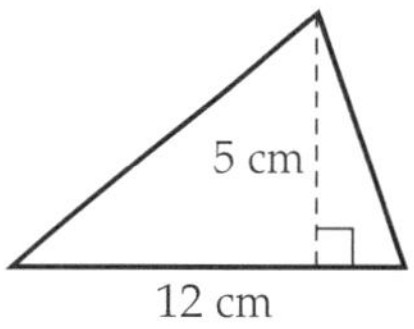

4 Find the area of this shape.

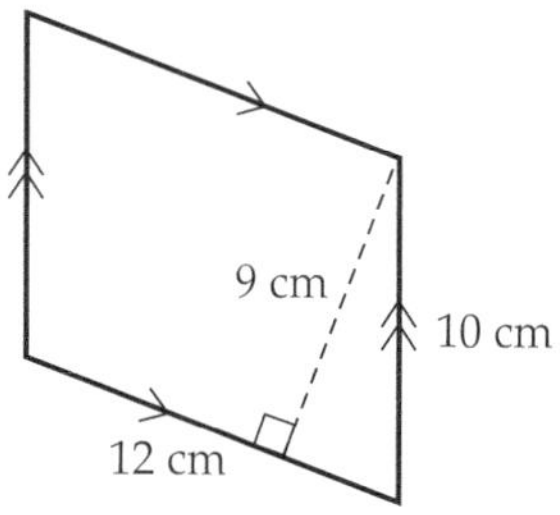

5 Calculate the area of this trapezium.

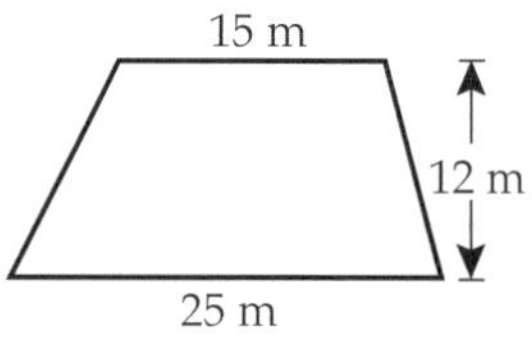

6 A rectangle is twice as long as it is wide. Its perimeter is 72 cm. What is the area of this rectangle?

7 Find the area of this circle, giving your answer correct to 2 decimal places.

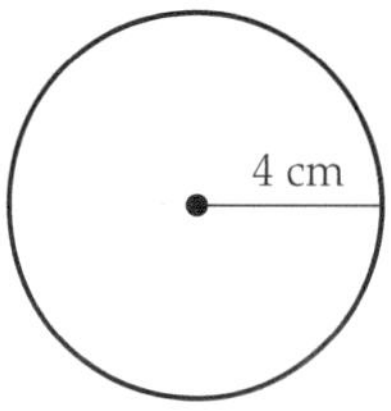

8 Find the area of this circle, giving your answer correct to 2 decimal places.

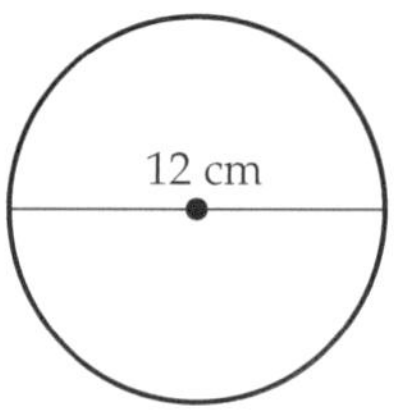

9 Aimie lost an earring in her classroom. She doesn't know in which direction it fell, but knows it couldn't have fallen more than a metre away from where she was standing. Assuming she is correct, how many square metres of carpet could she search to find her earring? Give your answer correct to 1 decimal place.

10 Find the area of the shaded shape correct to 2 decimal places.

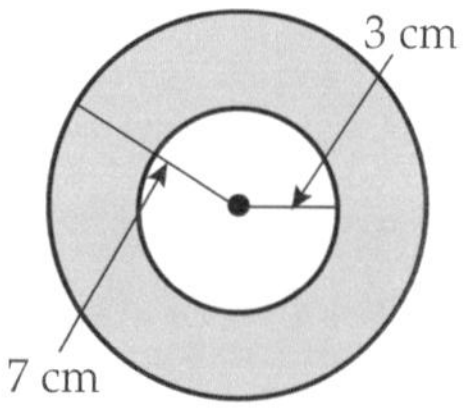

Practice 5B mark: /10

  ISBN 978 1 4886 1403 3

Pearson Mathematics 8 Homework Program

Measurement

Skills 5C

Skills & Practice: Total marks /27

Name: ....

Class: ....

Teacher: ....

This side of this worksheet reviews number skills. The other side of this worksheet refers to *Pearson Mathematics 8* Chapter 5 'Measurement' sections 5.6 and 5.7.

1 Complete the table below:

	12	-6	9	-3	-11	-7	4	-8	5
$\times 9$									

2 Complete the table below:

	-16	4	-18	8	22	-12	24	-20	6
$\div -2$									

3 Evaluate 356 000 ÷ 10 000.

4 Evaluate 539 × 400.

5 What are the next three numbers in the sequence?

3, 3, 5, 9, 15, 23, …

6 What is the next prime number after 35?

7 Evaluate (5 – 2) × (8 ÷ -2).

8 Evaluate $\frac{3}{14} - \frac{2}{21}$.

9 Arrange these decimals in ascending order.

21.12, 12.21, 21.21, 12.12, 12.02

10 What is 30 out of 60 as a percentage?

11 Evaluate 0.9 ÷ 0.3.

12 Simplify $2^2 \times 2^3$.

13 Solve this equation.

$$\frac{p+1}{3} = 2$$

14 If $t = -1$, find the value of $3t^2$.

15 Find the value of t in the diagram.

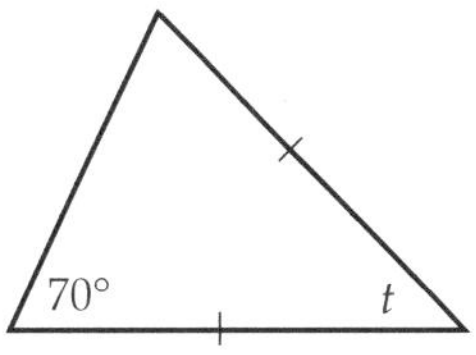

16 Two-up is a game in which two coins are tossed. What are the possible combinations for heads (H) and tails (T) shown on the two coins?

17 What is the area of this shape?

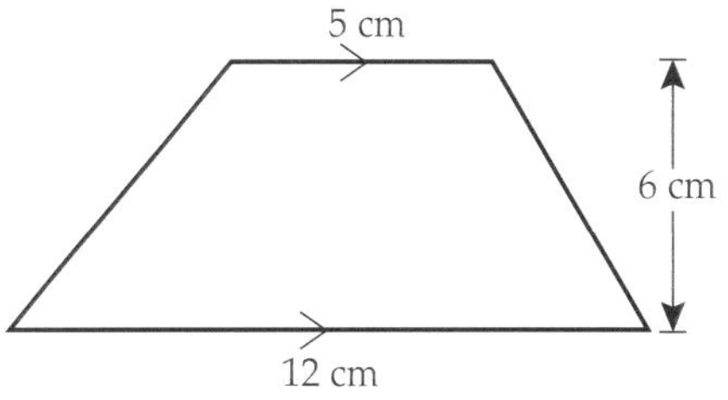

Skills 5C mark: /17

ISBN 978 1 4886 1403 3

Pearson Mathematics 8 Homework Program

Measurement

Practice 5C

Show all your working

This side of this worksheet covers *Pearson Mathematics 8* Chapter 5 'Measurement' sections 5.6 and 5.7.

For online help, go to your *Pearson Mathematics 8* eBook.

1 Find the area of the shape correct to 2 decimal places.

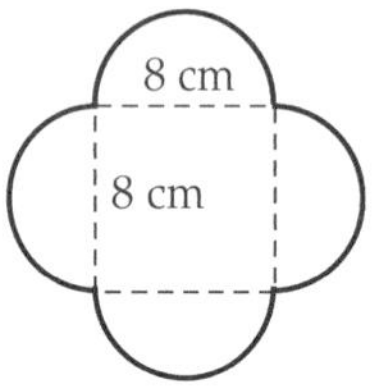

2 Find the area of the shaded shape correct to 2 decimal places.

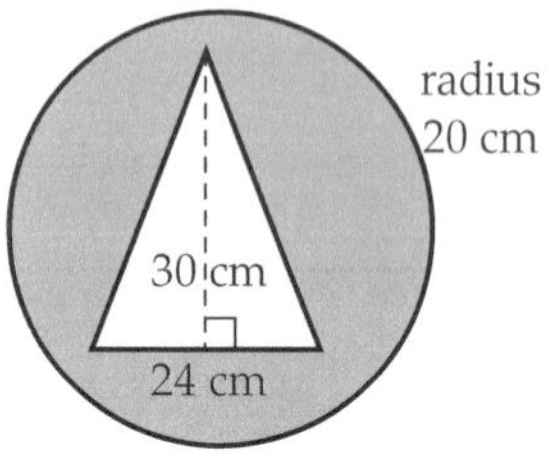

3 Find the area of the shaded shape correct to 2 decimal places.

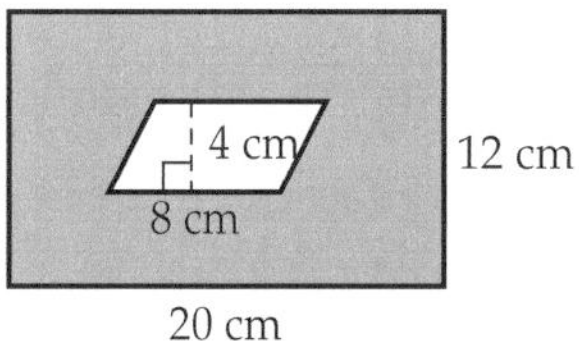

4 How much will it cost to cover the garden area below, with paving that costs \$20 per square metre?

Give your answer correct to the nearest whole dollar.

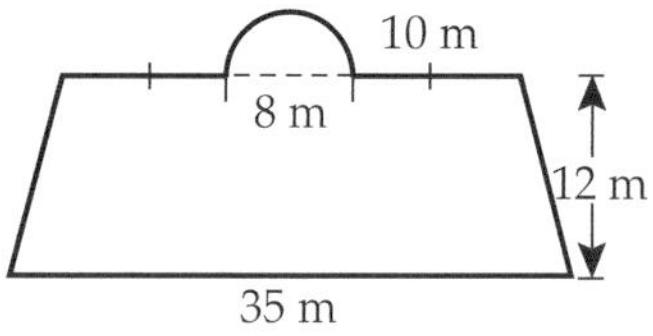

5 Find the volume of a square prism with base side length 20 cm and height 50 cm.

6 Find the volume of this prism.

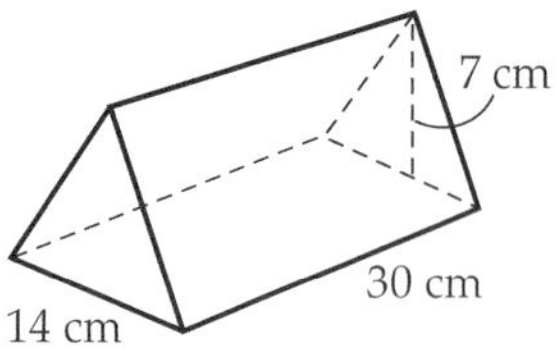

7 If the volume of this prism is 240 cm^3, what is the area of the shaded region?

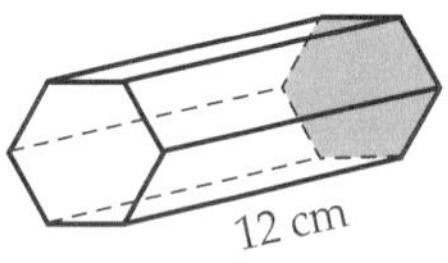

8 Calculate the capacity of the cylinder in litres, giving your answer correct to 2 decimal places.

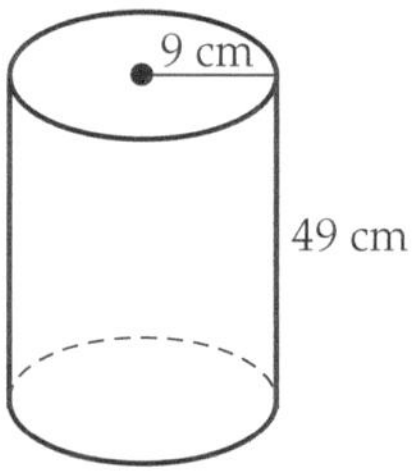

9 Convert 45 mL to cubic centimetres.

10 Convert 1250 mL to litres.

Practice 5C mark: /10

ISBN 978 1 4886 1403 3

Pearson Mathematics 8 Homework Program

Measurement

Skills 5D

Skills & Practice: Total marks /25

Name:

Class:

Teacher:

This side of this worksheet reviews number skills. The other side of this worksheet refers to *Pearson Mathematics 8* Chapter 5 'Measurement' section 5.8.

1 Complete the table below:

	9	-5	7	-11	4	6	-12	-3	8
− 8									

2 Complete the table below:

	-120	36	-12	24	-48	108	72	-132	60
÷ 12									

3 Evaluate $40.5 \div 100$.

4 Evaluate 721×40.

5 What are the next three numbers in the sequence?

1, 16, 81, 256, 625, …

6 Write 45 as a product of its prime factors in index form.

7 Evaluate $-4 + (-5 - 4) \div -3$.

8 Evaluate $1\frac{3}{4} - \frac{1}{2} - \frac{1}{3}$.

9 Insert a < or > symbol to make the expression true.

$\frac{11}{3}$ ☐ 3.6

10 What is the ratio of the number of millimetres in a metre to the number of centimetres in a metre?

11 Evaluate $2.2 \div 0.2$.

12 Evaluate 3×10^4.

13 Solve this equation.

$5r + 2 = r + 18$

14 If $x = 8$, find the value of $\sqrt{2x}$.

15 How many faces does an octagonal pyramid have?

16 Students in a class were surveyed on their favourite primary colour. What is the probability that the favourite primary colour of a randomly selected student is not red?

Colour	Frequency
Red	9
Yellow	7
Blue	11
Total	**27**

17 What is the volume of a cylinder that has a diameter of 7 cm and a height of 12 cm? Give your answer to the nearest whole number.

Skills 5D mark: /17

Pearson Mathematics 8 Homework Program

Measurement

Practice 5D

Show all your working

This side of this worksheet covers *Pearson Mathematics 8* Chapter 5 'Measurement' section 5.8.

For online help, go to your *Pearson Mathematics 8* eBook.

1 How much time has passed from 9:46 am to 4:30 pm?

2 Write the time 3:30 pm in 24-hour time.

3 Write the time 2140 in 12-hour (am/pm) time.

4 Perth's time zone is 2 hours behind Melbourne's time zone. What time is it in Perth when it is 1:30 pm in Melbourne?

5 Using the table below, calculate how much daily sunlight Venus will have (in hours and minutes).

Planet	Sunrise	Sunset
Mercury	7:02 am	9:26 pm
Venus	4:27 am	6:55 pm
Mars	1:01 am	12:44 pm

The table below shows equivalent times for the states and territories. Use it to help answer the next three questions.

State or Territory	Time
WA	9 am
SA, NT	10:30 am
Qld, NSW, Vic, Tas, ACT	11 am

6 Cindy's friend Linda lives in Perth. Cindy is in Melbourne and rings Linda at 7 am to say happy birthday. Suggest why Linda might be grumpy when she picks up the phone.

7 Cindy flies to Perth to visit Linda. The flight takes 4 hours and leaves at 1:50 pm Melbourne time. At what time will Cindy arrive, in Perth time?

8 Linda flies to Adelaide for a holiday. The flight takes 2 hours and leaves at 8:40 am Perth time. At what time will Linda arrive, in Adelaide time?

Practice 5D mark: /8

ISBN 978 1 4886 1403 3

Pearson Mathematics 8 Homework Program

Linear graphs

Skills 6A

Skills & Practice: Total marks /27

Name:

Class:

Teacher:

This side of this worksheet reviews number skills. The other side of this worksheet refers to *Pearson Mathematics 8* Chapter 6 'Linear graphs' sections 6.1 and 6.2.

1 Complete the table below:

	5	-12	-9	6	-8	3	-11	-7	-4
+ 8									

2 Complete the table below:

	54	-18	81	-63	27	99	-9	-72	36
÷ -9									

3 Evaluate $611 \div 100$.

4 Evaluate 5470×30.

5 What are the next three numbers in the sequence?

$0, \frac{1}{2}, \frac{2}{3}, \frac{3}{4}, \frac{4}{5}, \ldots$

6 List all the common factors of 45 and 18.

7 Evaluate $(-3 + -5) \times 4 + 20$.

8 Evaluate $\frac{1}{10} + \frac{3}{10} + \frac{7}{10}$.

9 Simplify $\frac{75}{6}$ and write as a mixed number.

10 Simplify the ratio 24:30:12.

11 Evaluate $22.49 + 28.55$.

12 Simplify $4f \times 3g \times 3h$.

13 Solve this equation.

$4(x - 3) = 24$

14 If $w = -3$, find the value of $w^2 + 1$.

15 Is a rectangle symmetrical?

16 Dan is training for a long distance running race and does a week of intensive running. On the seven days, he runs the following numbers of kilometres: 4, 5, 10, 3, 8, 5, 7. What is the average number of kilometres run per day?

17 The perimeter and area of a certain square have the same number value. What is the side length of this square?

Skills 6A mark: /17

ISBN 978 1 4886 1403 3

Pearson Mathematics Homework Program 8

Linear graphs

Practice 6A

Show all your working

This side of this worksheet covers *Pearson Mathematics 8* Chapter 6 'Linear graphs' sections 6.1 and 6.2.

For online help, go to your *Pearson Mathematics 8* eBook.

1 The graph represents the data for a baby in the first year of its life. What are the two variables in the graph?

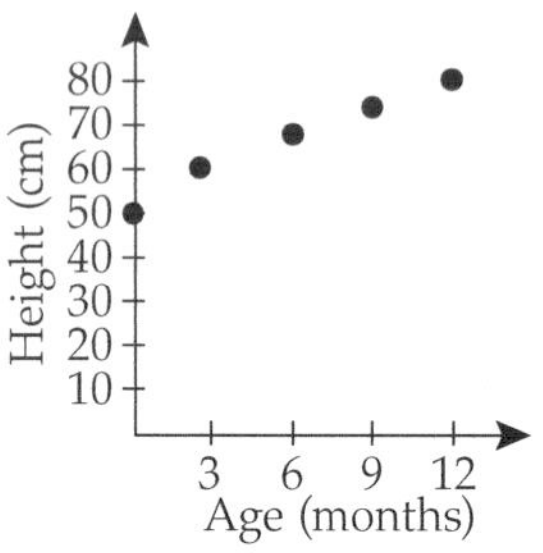

2 Does there seem to be a relationship between the two variables in the previous question? Describe the relationship.

3 Water is poured at a steady rate into a jug. The graph shows how the height of the water in the jug is related to time. Sketch the jug.

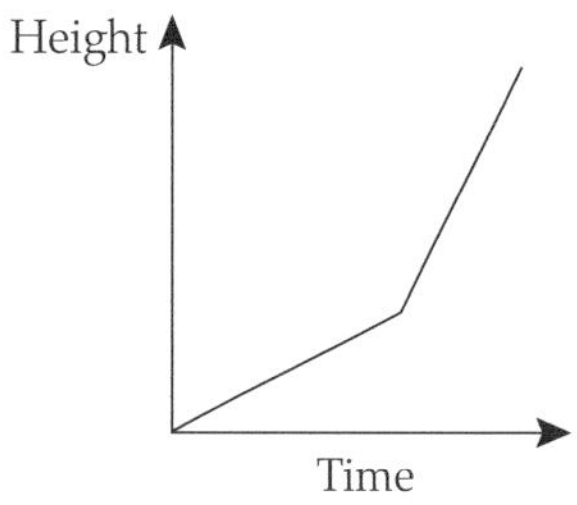

4 Water is poured at a steady rate into a jug with this shape. On the axes, sketch a graph to show how the height of the water is related to time.

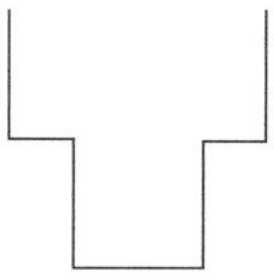

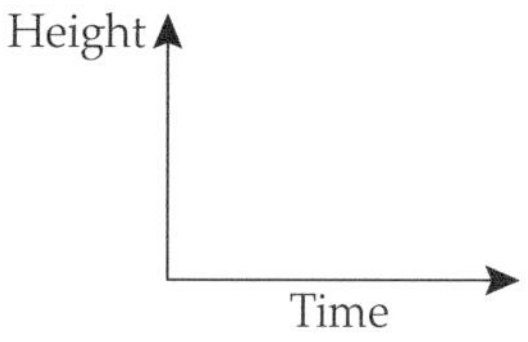

5 The graph shows Emily's distance from home while she is walking to school.

How far is school from her home?

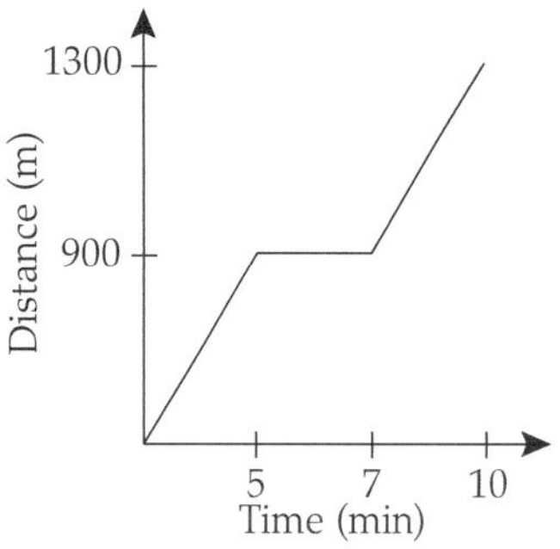

6 Use the rule $y = 4 - 2x$ to complete the table.

x	-2	0	1	3
y	8			
(x, y)	(-2, 8)			

7 Use the table from the previous question to draw the graph of the relationship $y = 4 - 2x$.

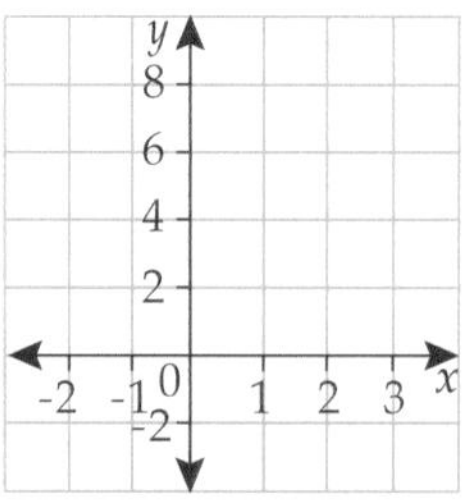

8 For the graph in the previous question, state the x-intercept and the y-intercept.

9 For the graph in the previous question, find the value of x where $y = -2$.

10 For the graph in the previous question, is the gradient positive or negative?

Practice 6A mark: /10

ISBN 978 1 4886 1403 3

Pearson Mathematics 8 Homework Program

Linear graphs

Skills 6B

Skills & Practice: Total marks /25

Name:

Class:

Teacher:

This side of this worksheet reviews number skills. The other side of this worksheet refers to *Pearson Mathematics 8* Chapter 6 'Linear graphs' section 6.3.

1 Complete the table below:

	3	-9	6	-12	4	8	-11	-5	7
× -4									

2 Complete the table below:

	-30	5	-45	35	-15	40	-25	55	-20
÷ 5									

3 Evaluate 3500 ÷ 1000.

4 Evaluate 1610 × 9.

5 What are the next three numbers in the sequence?

$1, \frac{1}{2}, \frac{1}{4}, \frac{1}{8}, \frac{1}{16}, \ldots$

6 Write 108 as a product of its prime factors in index form.

7 Evaluate -2 × (13 − 9) ÷ -4.

8 Evaluate $1\frac{5}{7} \div 1\frac{1}{3}$.

9 What is 0.001 55 rounded to 4 decimal places?

10 Write 85% as a fraction in simplest form.

11 Evaluate 0.7 × 0.8.

12 Simplify $6m \div 3m$.

13 Solve this equation.

$\frac{x}{5} - 3 = 2$

14 Simplify $g^2 + 4g + 5 - 3g + g^2$.

15 Find the value of the angle *a* in this diagram.

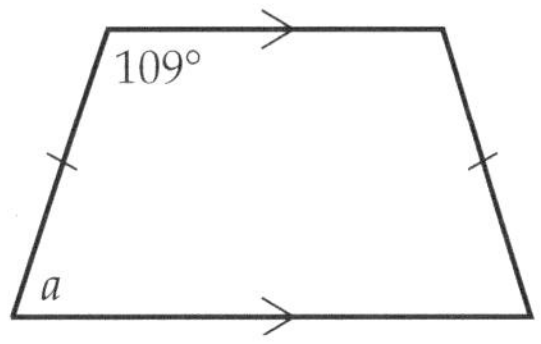

16 What is the probability of getting a red 7 from a standard pack of 52 playing cards?

17 Find the perimeter of this triangle, giving your answer to 2 decimal places.

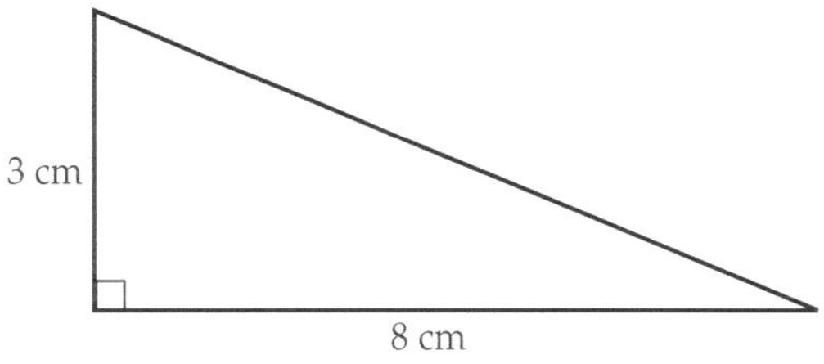

Skills 6B mark: /17

ISBN 978 1 4886 1403 3

Pearson Mathematics 8 Homework Program

Linear graphs

Practice 6B

This side of this worksheet covers *Pearson Mathematics 8* Chapter 6 'Linear graphs' section 6.3.

For online help, go to your *Pearson Mathematics 8* eBook.

1 Find the rule for this set of points.

(-3, 2), (-2, 2), (-1, 2), (0, 2), (1, 2), (2, 2)

2 Find the rule for this set of points.

(-1, 4), (0, 2), (1, 0), (2, -2)

3 Using your answer to the previous question, find the missing information for the following point.

(3, ___)

4 Find the rule for the relationship shown between x and y.

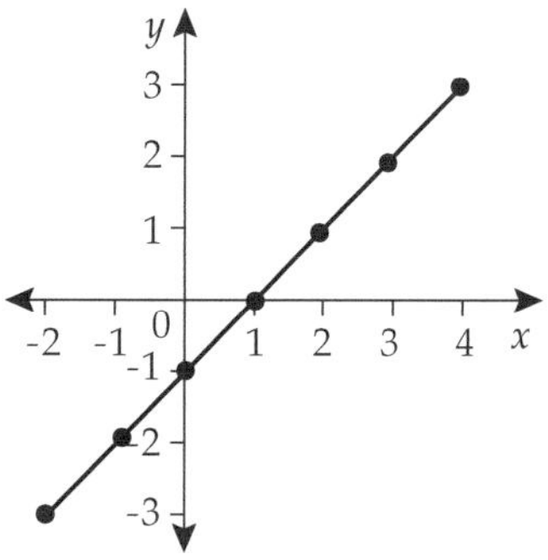

5 Find the rule for this table of values.

x	-3	-1	0	2
y	-1	1	2	4

6 Use the fact that 3 metres is approximately equal to 10 feet to draw an approximate conversion graph on this grid for distances up to 3 metres.

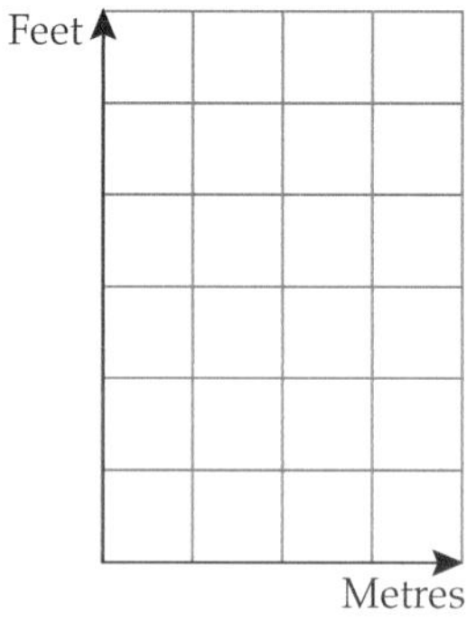

7 Use the graph in the previous question to approximately convert this length.

6 feet ≈ ___ metres

8 Use the graph in the previous question to approximately convert this length.

1 metre ≈ ___ feet

Practice 6B mark: /18

ISBN 978 1 4886 1403 3

Pearson Mathematics 8 Homework Program

Linear graphs

Skills 6C

Skills & Practice: Total marks /25

Name:

Class:

Teacher:

This side of this worksheet reviews number skills. The other side of this worksheet refers to *Pearson Mathematics 8* Chapter 6 'Linear graphs' section 6.4.

1 Complete the table below:

	6	-9	5	-12	7	-4	11	-3	8
$\times 5$									

2 Complete the table below:

	-64	16	-48	32	-72	56	-24	96	-40
$\div$ -8									

3 Evaluate 2.03×100.

4 Evaluate $3250 \div 50$.

5 What are the next three numbers in the sequence?

2, 8, 13, 17, 20, 22, …

6 What is the highest common factor of 56 and 49?

7 Evaluate $(2 + -4) \times -3 - (3 \times -5)$.

8 Evaluate $\frac{1}{2} + \frac{1}{3} + \frac{1}{6}$.

9 Simplify $\frac{147}{9}$ and write as a mixed number.

10 Simplify the ratio 25 : 35 : 50.

11 Evaluate $0.123 + 0.987$.

12 Evaluate $30mn \div 6m$.

13 Solve this equation.

$$\frac{x+1}{5} = 2$$

14 If $b = -5$ and $c = -4$, find the value of $\frac{4b}{c}$.

15 What special type of quadrilateral has only one pair of parallel sides?

16 Inside a bag are five different shapes: a square, a rectangle, a rhombus, a parallelogram and a trapezium. What is the probability that a randomly selected shape will have two pairs of parallel sides?

17 Find the area of this shape.

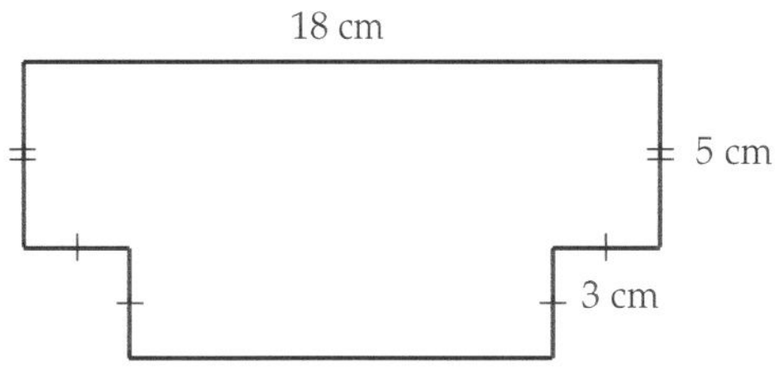

Skills 6C mark: /17

ISBN 978 1 4886 1403 3

Pearson Mathematics 8 Homework Program

Linear graphs

Practice 6C

Show all your working

This side of this worksheet covers *Pearson Mathematics 8* Chapter 6 'Linear graphs' section 6.4.

For online help, go to your *Pearson Mathematics 8* eBook.

1 Rick was edging his garden with wood that cost \$3 per metre.

Use this information to complete the table.

Length of wood (m)	0	1	2	3	4
Cost (\$)					

2 Using the table in the previous question, plot a graph of this relationship.
Use the horizontal axis to represent the length of wood.

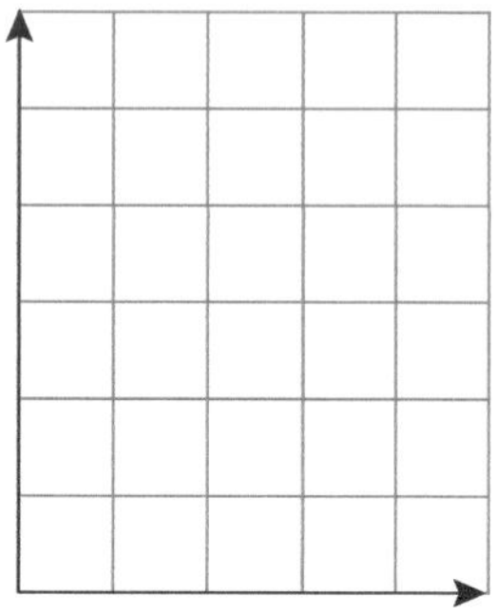

Use the table in the first question and the graph in the second question to answer Questions 3–6.

3 Is the relationship in the table and graph linear?

4 How much would 2.5 m of wood cost?

5 How much wood could be bought for \$10.50?

6 How much wood could be bought for \$15?

7 An electrician charges a callout fee and then a fixed amount for each hour it takes to finish the job.

Write an equation to represent the total cost of the electrician's work.

8 In the previous question, is there a linear relationship between the total cost and the hours of work?

Practice 6C mark: /8

  ISBN 978 1 4886 1403 3

Pearson Mathematics 8 Homework Program

Linear equations

Skills 7A

Skills & Practice: Total marks /27

Name:

Class:

Teacher:

This side of this worksheet reviews number skills. The other side of this worksheet refers to *Pearson Mathematics 8* Chapter 7 'Linear equations' sections 7.1 and 7.2.

1 Complete the table below:

	-5	7	11	-6	-9	4	-10	-8	12
− 7									

2 Complete the table below:

	120	-36	12	-240	48	-108	72	-132	60
÷ -12									

3 Evaluate 25.9×10.

4 Evaluate $9000 \div 3$.

5 What are the next two numbers in the sequence?
1, 21, 321, 4321, 54 321, …

6 What is the highest common factor of 36 and 48?

7 Evaluate $(8 - 3) \times (-2 + -4)$.

8 Evaluate $\frac{1}{9} + \frac{7}{18}$.

9 Arrange the following in ascending order.
$0.13, \frac{1}{9}, 0.1, \frac{1}{8}$

10 Simplify the ratio 60:72.

11 Evaluate $1.350 - 0.276$.

12 Write 5^6 in expanded form.

13 Solve this equation.
$x - 5 = 12$

14 If $q = 2$, find the value of $q(q + 1)$.

15 How many vertices does a cube have?

16 In Steve's last four cricket matches, he made 52 runs, 70 runs, 26 runs and 44 runs. How many runs did Steve make on average?

17 The length of a particular rectangle is twice its width. What is the length of this rectangle if the area is 98 cm^2?

Skills 7A mark: /17

ISBN 978 1 4886 1403 3

Pearson Mathematics 8 Homework Program

Linear equations

Practice 7A

This side of this worksheet covers *Pearson Mathematics 8* Chapter 7 'Linear equations' sections 7.1 and 7.2.

For online help, go to your *Pearson Mathematics 8* eBook.

1 Write an equation for the following.
Use x to represent the unknown number.
'A number is doubled and 3 is added.
The result is 18.'

2 Write an equation for the following.
Use b to represent the unknown number.
'A number is subtracted from 20 and 3 is added.
The result is 11.'

3 Is $f = 2$ a solution to $14 + f = 16$?

4 Solve this equation.
$3x - 3 = 33$

5 Solve this equation.
$3(a - 3) = 3$

6 Solve this equation.
$\frac{x}{3} - 3 = 3$

7 Solve this equation.
$\frac{c-3}{3} = 3$

8 Use the graph of $y = 3x - 2$ to solve $3x - 2 = 4$.

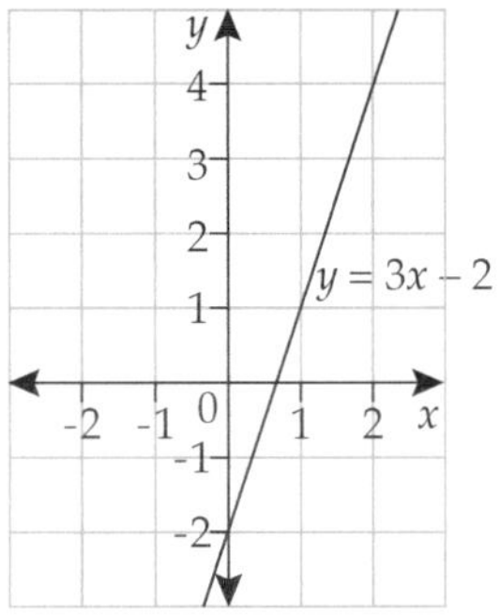

9 Solve this equation.
$10 - 5n = 20$

10 Riley's age is twice her brother's age plus two years. If Riley is fourteen years old, how old is her brother?

Practice 7A mark: /10

  ISBN 978 1 4886 1403 3

Pearson Mathematics 8 Homework Program

Linear equations

Skills 7B

Skills & Practice: Total marks /27

Name:

Class:

Teacher:

This side of this worksheet reviews number skills. The other side of this worksheet refers to *Pearson Mathematics 8* Chapter 7 'Linear equations' sections 7.3 and 7.4.

1 Complete the table below:

	5	-7	11	-6	9	4	-10	8	-12
$\times$ 12									

2 Complete the table below:

	-80	120	-100	30	10	-90	40	-60	110
$\div$ -10									

3 Evaluate 179.6×100.

4 Evaluate $12\,000 \div 6$.

5 What is the next number in the sequence?

1, 121, 12 321, 1 234 321, …

6 What is the lowest common multiple of 84 and 56?

7 Evaluate $-2 + (4 - -3) \times -3$.

8 Evaluate $2\frac{2}{5} \times 3\frac{3}{4}$.

9 What is 0.003 73 rounded to 4 decimal places?

10 What is 25% of \$12?

11 Evaluate 0.8×0.5.

12 Simplify $2x \times 3y \div 6x$.

13 Solve this equation.

$9x - 5 = 22$

14 Simplify $-9j + 4jk - 3jk + 12j$.

15 Hamish has made a mistake in the points he has plotted. When the points are in their correct positions, a line can be drawn through them and the origin.

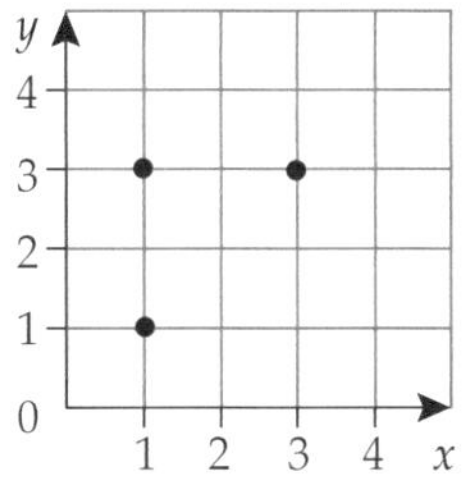

Which point should be moved? (Write its coordinates.)

To where should it be moved?

16 What is the probability of rolling a prime number on a standard six-sided die?

17 Find the area of this shape correct to two decimal places.

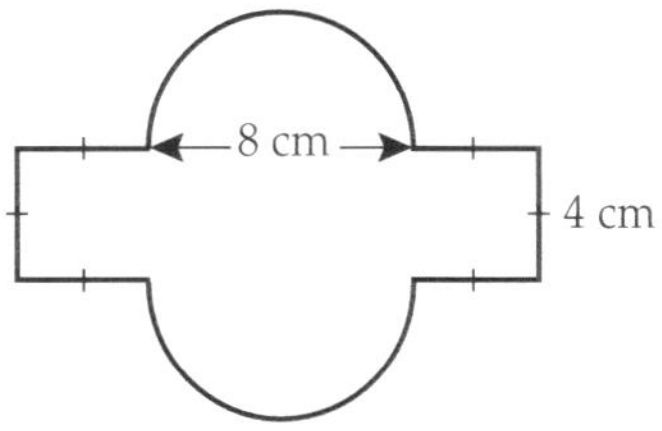

Skills 7B mark: /17

ISBN 978 1 4886 1403 3

Pearson Mathematics Homework Program 8

Linear equations

Practice 7B

Show all your working

This side of this worksheet covers *Pearson Mathematics 8* Chapter 7 'Linear equations' sections 7.3 and 7.4.

For online help, go to your *Pearson Mathematics 8* eBook.

1 Solve this equation.

$$\frac{d}{3} + 4 = 13$$

2 Solve for h.

$$\frac{h-2}{4} = 3$$

3 Solve for x.

$$\frac{2x-1}{5} = 3$$

4 Solve this equation.

$$\frac{4b}{5} - 1 = 3$$

5 Solve for x.

$$\frac{3x-3}{3} + 3 = -3$$

6 Solve for r.

$$3r + 5 = 2r + 7$$

7 Solve the following equation graphically to find the point of intersection.

$$2x + 7 = 3x + 3$$

8 Solve this equation.

$$2(m + 5) = 3(m + 3)$$

9 Solve for x.

$$5(3x - 2) = 4(2x + 1)$$

10 Seven times a certain number, minus four, gives the same result as nine times that certain number, minus six. Write an equation and solve it to find the unknown number.

Practice 7B mark: /10

ISBN 978 1 4886 1403 3

Pearson Mathematics 8 Homework Program

Linear equations

Skills 7C

Skills & Practice: Total marks /27

Name: ....

Class: ....

Teacher: ....

This side of this worksheet reviews number skills. The other side of this worksheet refers to *Pearson Mathematics 8* Chapter 7 'Linear equations' section 7.5.

1 Complete the table below:

	5	-11	7	-3	12	-9	4	-8	6
− 11									

2 Complete the table below:

	21	-6	24	-12	36	18	-9	27	-15
÷ 3									

3 Evaluate 65.88×10.

4 Evaluate $2400 \div 80$.

5 What are the next two numbers in the sequence?

1, 11, 101, 1001, 10 001, …

6 Express 90 as a product of its prime factors in index form.

7 Evaluate $(9 + -5) \div (8 \div -2)$.

8 Evaluate $1\frac{3}{5} - 1\frac{1}{3}$.

9 Insert a < or > symbol to make the expression true.

$\frac{17}{4}$ ☐ 4.1

10 Simplify the ratio 210 : 140.

11 Evaluate $2.4 \div 0.6$.

12 Simplify $3d^2 \times 3c$.

13 Solve for x.

$9(x - 4) = 18$

14 If $a = -4$ and $b = -2$, find the value of $3ab$.

15 Find the value of the angle z in this diagram.

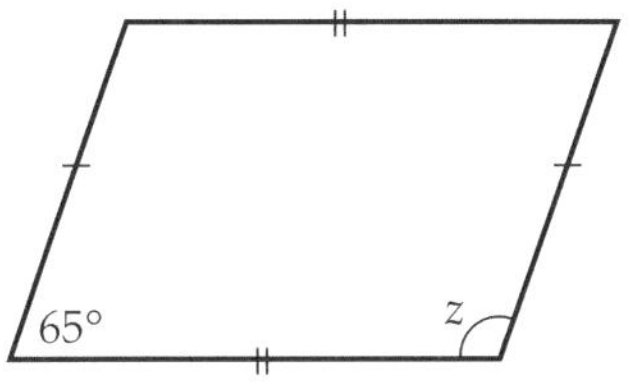

16 A class was surveyed to find their favourite day of the school week. The results were put into a frequency table.

Day	Frequency
Monday	1
Tuesday	6
Wednesday	7
Thursday	4
Friday	12
Total	**30**

What was the most common response?

17 Find the volume of this block.

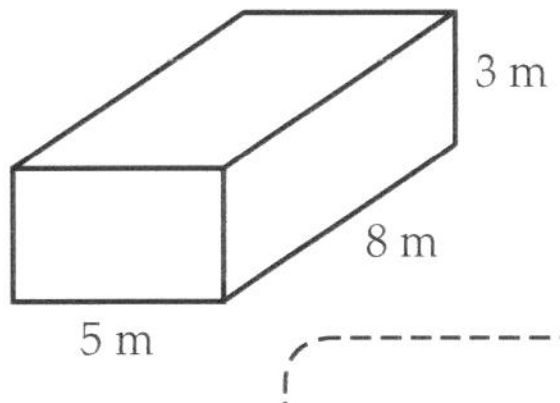

Skills 7C mark: /17

ISBN 978 1 4886 1403 3

Pearson Mathematics 8 Homework Program

Linear equations

Practice 7C

Show all your working

This side of this worksheet covers *Pearson Mathematics 8* Chapter 7 'Linear equations' section 7.5.

For online help, go to your *Pearson Mathematics 8* eBook.

1 Write an equation to represent the following situation.

A class has 23 students. If they enter a classroom and find that there are five more students than chairs, how many chairs are in the room?

2 Solve the equation in the previous question.

3 Write an equation to represent the following.

Dina bought a salad roll and milkshake for lunch. The cost of the salad roll is $\$x$ and the milkshake costs \$2.50. In total, Dina spent \$5.30.

4 Solve the equation in the previous question to find the cost of the salad roll.

5 Write an equation to represent the following. Use x to represent the width.

A rectangle is 5 cm longer than it is wide. Its perimeter is 18 cm.

6 Solve the equation in the previous question to find the width of the rectangle.

7 Write an equation to represent the following. Use b to represent the length of one side.

The perimeter of a square is 18 cm.

8 Solve the equation in the previous question to find the length of one side.

9 Write an equation to represent the following.

In a game of basketball, the Knights scored 16 more points than the Supercats. The total points scored was 130.

10 Solve the equation in the previous question to find the number of points scored by the Supercats.

Practice 7C mark: /10

ISBN 978 1 4886 1403 3

Pearson Mathematics 8 Homework Program

Geometry

Skills 8A

Skills & Practice: Total marks /27

Name:

Class:

Teacher:

This side of this worksheet reviews number skills. The other side of this worksheet refers to *Pearson Mathematics 8* Chapter 8 'Geometry' section 8.1.

1 Complete the table below:

	-8	3	-6	11	-4	9	-5	12	-7
$\times 3$									

2 Complete the table below:

	88	-22	110	-44	121	-33	55	-132	77
$\div$ -11									

3 Evaluate 23.55×1000.

4 Evaluate $33\,200 \div 20$.

5 What are the next three numbers in the sequence?

1, -2, 4, -8, 16, …

6 What is the lowest common multiple of 15 and 18?

7 Evaluate $-2 \times -3 + 4 \times -5 - 5 \times -6$.

8 Evaluate $3\frac{3}{4} \times 1\frac{3}{5}$.

9 What is 0.4026 rounded to 3 decimal places?

10 Express 42% as a fraction in simplest form.

11 Evaluate 0.08×3.

12 Evaluate $6mn \div 3mn$.

13 Solve this equation.

$5 + 3x = 29$

14 If $x = 25$, find the value of $\sqrt{x}$.

15 Find the value of the angle s in the diagram.

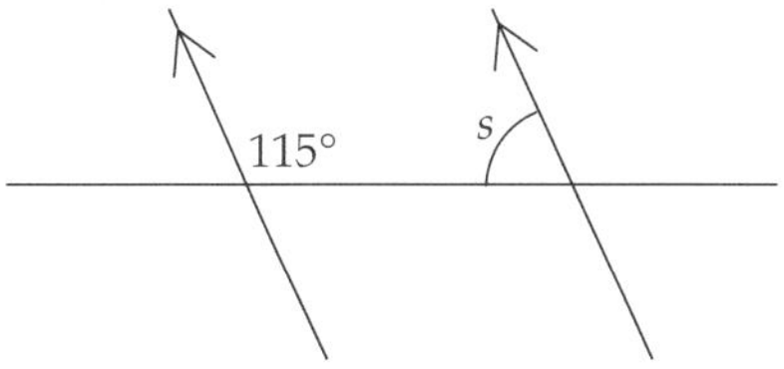

16 Find the median of these shoe sizes.

$6, 7\frac{1}{2}, 8, 7, 7\frac{1}{2}, 6, 5, 9, 7$

17 A rectangular swimming pool is 4 m wide and 10.5 m long and has a depth of 1.8 m. What is its volume?

Skills 8A mark: /17

ISBN 978 1 4886 1403 3

Pearson Mathematics Homework Program 8

Geometry

Practice 8A

Show all your working

This side of this worksheet covers *Pearson Mathematics 8* Chapter 8 'Geometry' section 8.1.

For online help, go to your *Pearson Mathematics 8* eBook.

1 What is the complement of 27°?

2 What is the supplement of 86°?

3 Which angle is alternate to angle *d*?

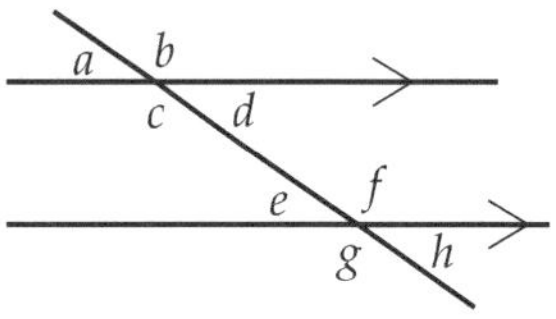

4 Find the size of the angle *c*.

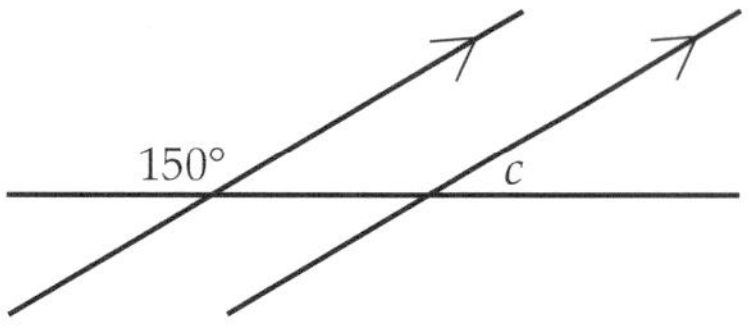

5 Find the value of the angle *x*. Give reasons for your answer.

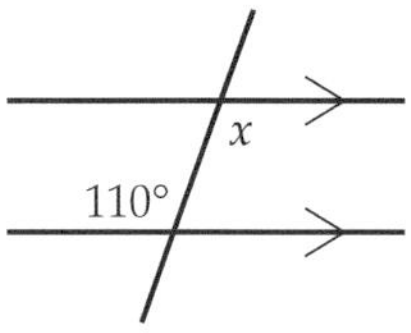

6 Find the size of the angle *d*.

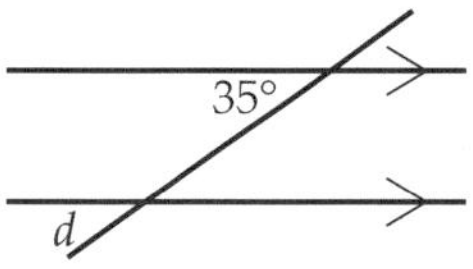

7 Find the value of the pronumeral *x*. Give reasons for your answer.

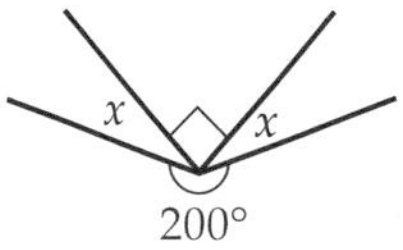

8 Find the value of *b* in the diagram.

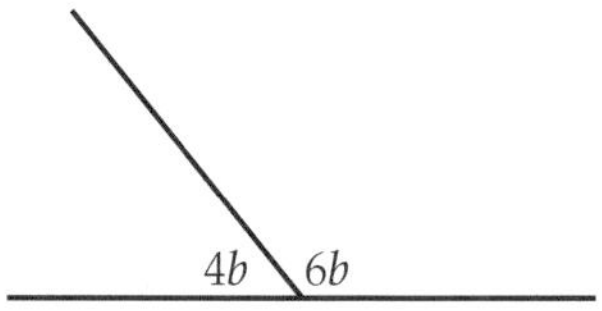

9 Find the value of the pronumeral *x* in this diagram. Give reasons for your answer.

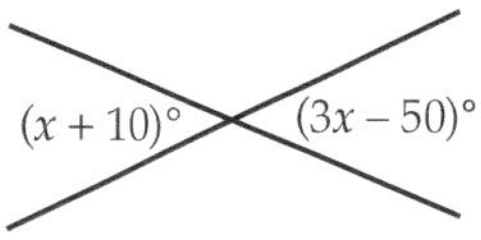

10 Riley is at the top of a grandstand at the MCG. She looks straight ahead and then down at an angle of 32°. She sees the back of the head of her friend Reuben, who is sitting in the first row. She calls Reuben and tells him that he should turn around, look straight ahead, then move his head up a certain angle and he will see Riley. What is this angle?

Practice 8A mark: /10

ISBN 978 1 4886 1403 3

Pearson Mathematics 8 Homework Program

Geometry

Skills 8B

Skills & Practice: Total marks /27

Name: ....

Class: ....

Teacher: ....

This side of this worksheet reviews number skills. The other side of this worksheet refers to *Pearson Mathematics 8* Chapter 8 'Geometry' section 8.2.

1 Complete the table below:

	10	-2	12	7	-4	9	-11	6	-8
× 5									

2 Complete the table below:

	-12	40	-28	8	-48	12	16	-24	32
÷ -4									

3 Evaluate 0.5 ÷ 10.

4 Evaluate 257 × 70.

5 What are the next three numbers in the sequence?

$1, \frac{1}{4}, \frac{1}{9}, \frac{1}{16}, \frac{1}{25}, \ldots$

6 What is the highest common factor of 108 and 240?

7 Evaluate (3 + 9) ÷ (2 – 5) × -2.

8 Evaluate $\frac{1}{4} + \frac{1}{6} + \frac{1}{3}$.

9 Simplify $\frac{84}{8}$ and express as a mixed number.

10 Simplify the ratio 25% : 60% : 15%.

11 Evaluate 12.1 – 1.52.

12 Simplify $12stu \div 3st$.

13 Solve this equation.

$\frac{x-6}{4} = 3$

14 If $a = 7$ and $b = 2$, find the value of a^b.

15 Find the value of x in this diagram.

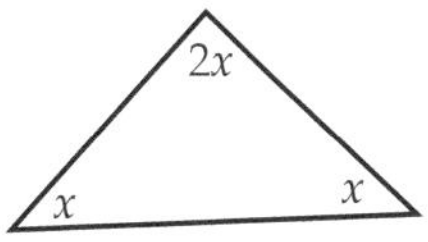

16 How many faces does a die have, if the probability of rolling a 4 is $\frac{1}{5}$ and 4 only appears once?

17 What is the area of this shape?

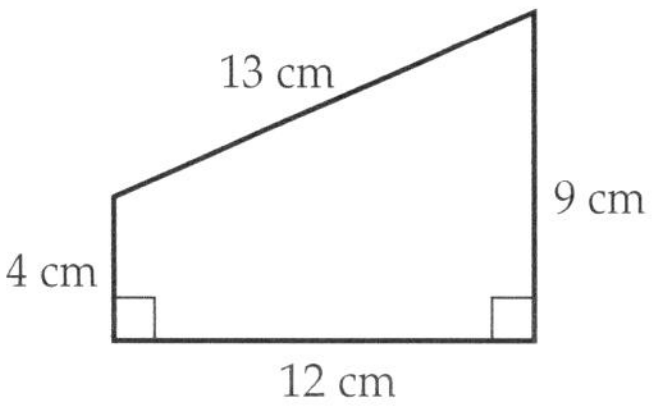

Skills 8B mark: /17

Pearson Mathematics Homework Program

8

Geometry

Practice 8B

Show all your working

This side of this worksheet covers *Pearson Mathematics 8* Chapter 8 'Geometry' section 8.2.

For online help, go to your *Pearson Mathematics 8* eBook.

1 Find the value of c.

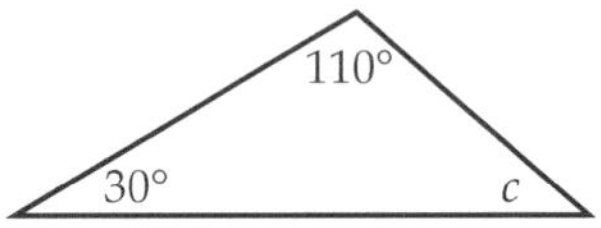

2 Find the value of d.

3 What is the most appropriate name for this quadrilateral?

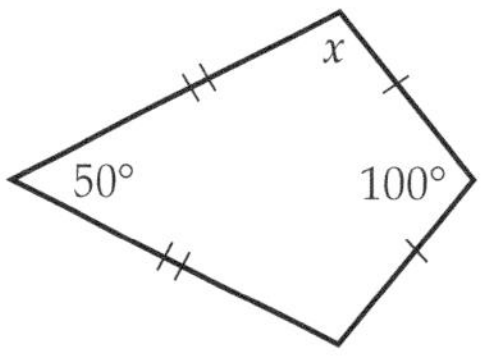

4 Find the value of x in the previous question.

5 True or false? A square is an example of a rhombus.

6 Find the value of the angle x. Give reasons for your answer.

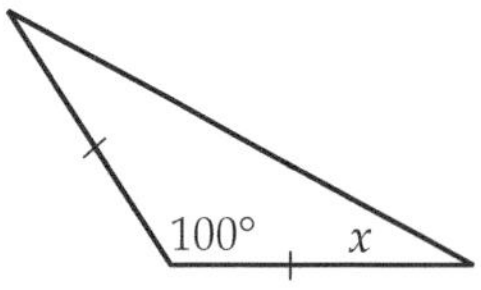

7 Find the value of the pronumeral. Give reasons for your answer.

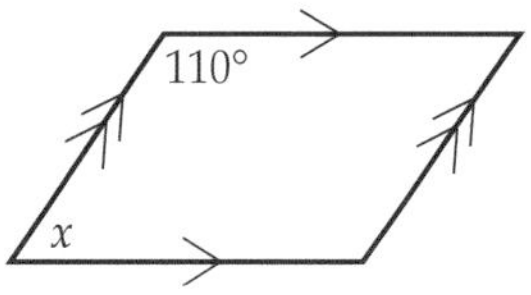

8 Find the value of the pronumeral. Give reasons for your answer.

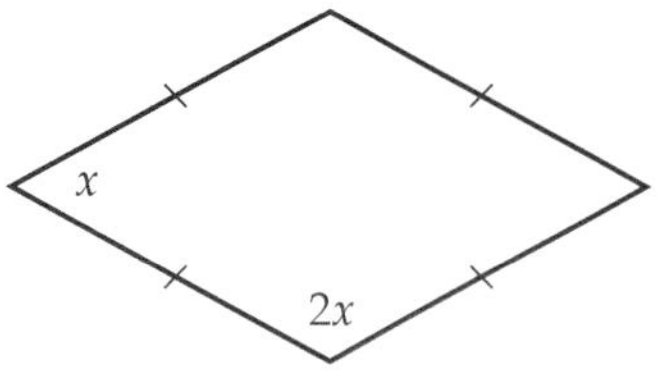

9 Find the value of the pronumeral. Give reasons for your answer.

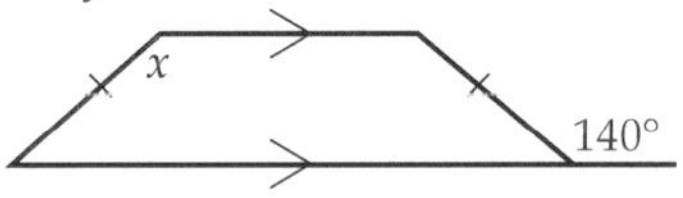

10 Find the value of the pronumeral. Give reasons for your answer.

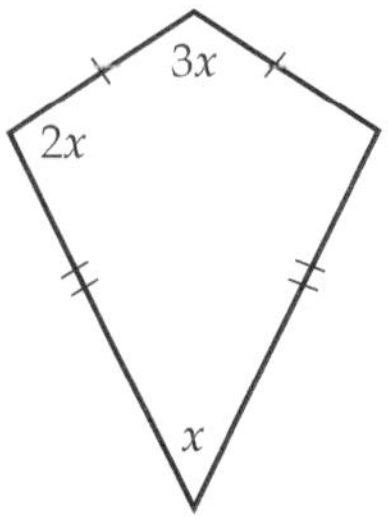

Practice 8B mark: /10

ISBN 978 1 4886 1403 3

Pearson Mathematics 8 Homework Program

Geometry

Skills 8C

Skills & Practice: Total marks /25

Name:

Class:

Teacher:

This side of this worksheet reviews number skills. The other side of this worksheet refers to *Pearson Mathematics 8* Chapter 8 'Geometry' sections 8.3, 8.4 and 8.5.

1 Complete the table below:

	-8	5	-9	4	-7	3	-12	2	-6
+ 9									

2 Complete the table below:

	-56	21	63	-35	-14	42	-84	28	-49
÷ 7									

3 Evaluate $9.6 \div 100$.

4 Evaluate 342×60.

5 What are the next three numbers in the sequence?

1, 3, 9, 27, …

6 What is the lowest common multiple of 16 and 24?

7 Evaluate $(6 - -5) - 12 \div (1 - 5)$.

8 Evaluate $1\frac{1}{6} \div 3\frac{1}{9}$.

9 What is 0.080 808 rounded to 3 decimal places?

10 Express 65% as a fraction in simplest form.

11 Evaluate 0.04×6.

12 Evaluate $(2)^3$.

13 Solve this equation.

$$\frac{3x + 2}{4} = 5$$

14 Simplify $1.5p + 0.4p - 0.3p$.

15 Find the value of x.

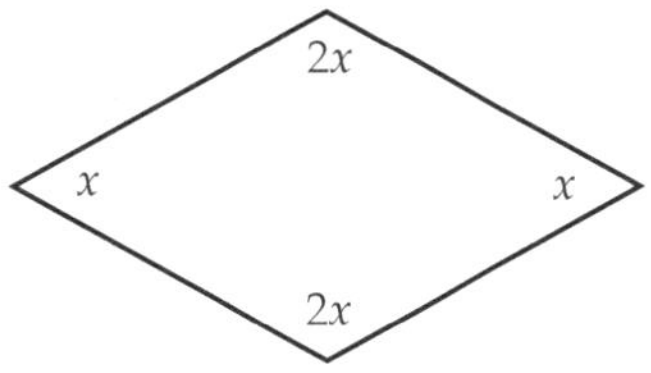

16 What is the probability of rolling a number greater than 3 on a standard six-sided die?

17 What is the circumference of a circle that has a diameter of 7 cm? Give your answer to 1 decimal place.

Skills 8C mark: /17

ISBN 978 1 4886 1403 3

Pearson Mathematics Homework Program 8

Geometry

Practice 8C

Show all your working

This side of this worksheet covers *Pearson Mathematics 8* Chapter 8 'Geometry' sections 8.3, 8.4 and 8.5.

For online help, go to your *Pearson Mathematics 8* eBook.

1

a Describe the translation needed to place the shape *ABCDE* on top of the second shape.

b Label the second figure using the appropriate notation.

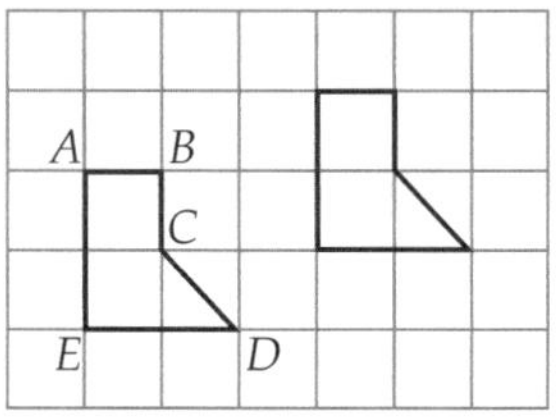

2

For the congruent statement $ADFG \equiv ZYVT$ complete the following pairings:

a $F \leftrightarrow$

b $FG \leftrightarrow$

b $\angle AGF \leftrightarrow$

3

Write a congruence statement for the pair of congruent figures below.

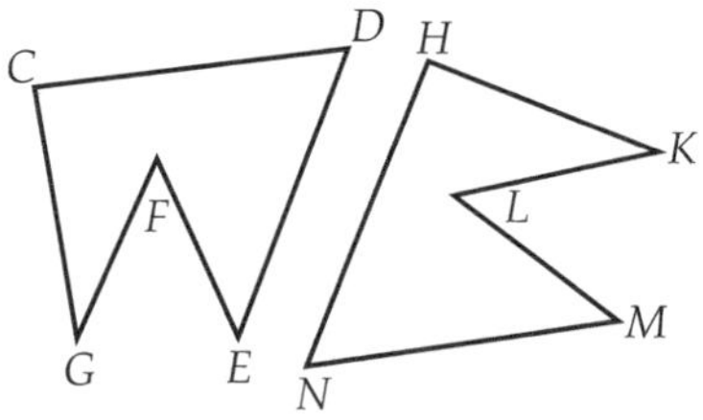

4

State what test you would use to show that the following triangles are congruent.

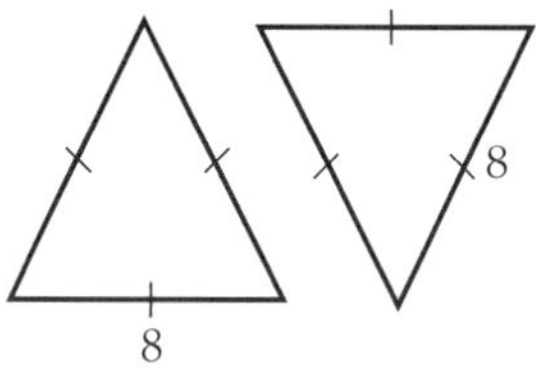

5

Give a reason why this pair of triangles is congruent.

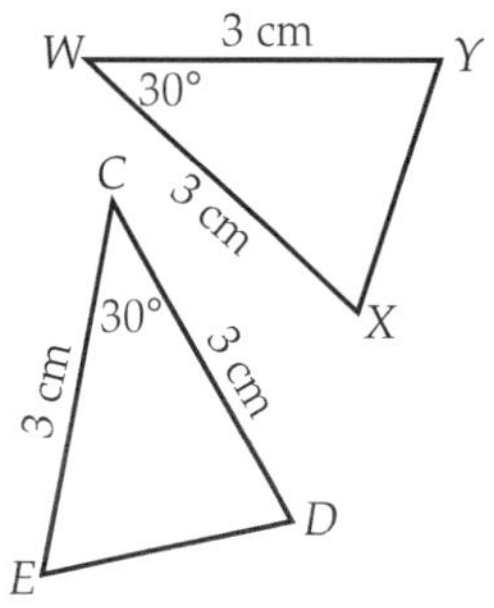

6

This figure is a parallelogram. Name any pairs of congruent triangles you can find.

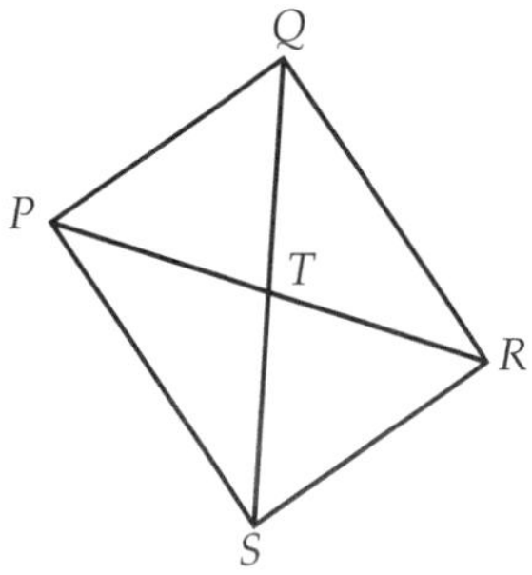

7

Use congruent triangles to prove that the opposite angles shown in the shape below are equal.

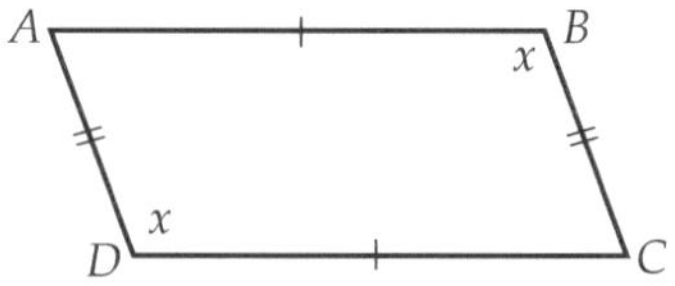

8

Use congruent triangles and known angle facts to find the value of the pronumeral x.

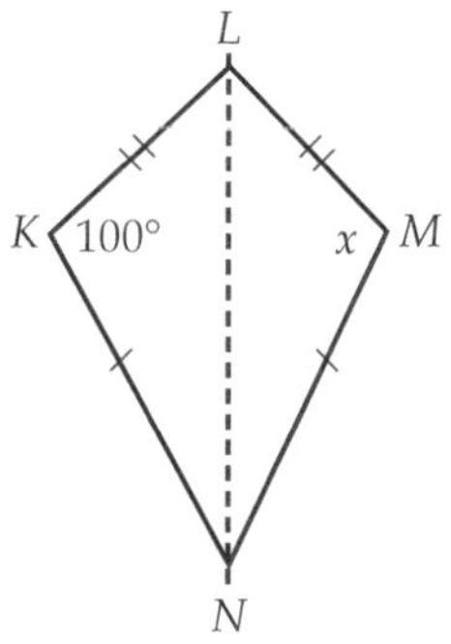

Practice 8C mark: /18

ISBN 978 1 4886 1403 3

Pearson Mathematics 8 Homework Program

Statistics and probability

Skills 9A

Skills & Practice: Total marks /23

Name: ....

Class: ....

Teacher: ....

This side of this worksheet reviews number skills. The other side of this worksheet refers to *Pearson Mathematics 8* Chapter 9 'Statistics and probability' sections 9.1, 9.2 and 9.3.

1 Complete the table below:

	5	-7	11	-6	9	-4	10	8	-12
× -11									

2 Complete the table below:

	-77	21	-35	7	140	-42	700	-49	280
÷ 7									

3 Evaluate 0.005×100.

4 Evaluate $25\,800 \div 300$.

5 What are the next two numbers in the sequence?

5, 5, 10, 30, 120, …

6 Is 12 a factor of 672?

7 Evaluate $-9 \times 8 + 7 \times -6 - 5 \times -4 - 3 \times -2$.

8 Evaluate $1\frac{1}{5} + 2\frac{1}{2} + 2\frac{1}{4}$.

9 Simplify $\frac{150}{12}$ and write as a mixed number.

10 Express 88% as a fraction in simplest form.

11 Evaluate $12.89 - 9.27$.

12 Simplify $5p \times 2q \div 4p$.

13 Solve this equation.

$5h + 6 = 12 - h$

14 If $x = 98$, find the value of $\sqrt{\frac{x}{2}}$.

15 If the following points form a line when joined, which point is the y-intercept of the line?

(1, 3), (2, 4), (0, 2), (-2, 0)

16 What is the probability that a card selected at random from a standard pack of 52 playing cards will be even-numbered?

17 What is the volume of this prism?

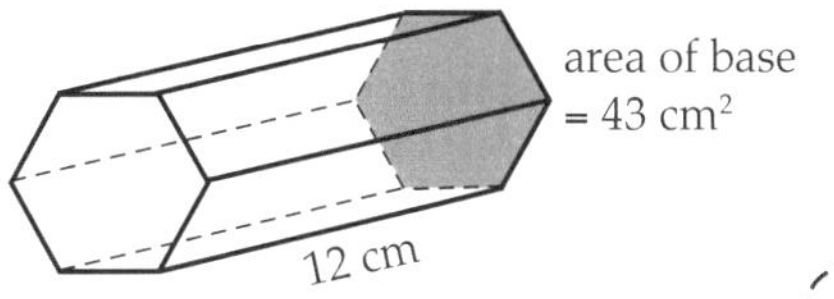

Skills 9A mark: /17

ISBN 978 1 4886 1403 3

Pearson Mathematics Homework Program 8

Statistics and probability

Practice 9A

Show all your working

This side of this worksheet covers *Pearson Mathematics 8* Chapter 9 'Statistics and probability' sections 9.1, 9.2 and 9.3.

For online help, go to your *Pearson Mathematics 8* eBook.

1 Year 8 students were trying to find the average number of pets per household in their local area, so they surveyed all the customers at the local vet clinic. Give a reason why this survey method might be biased.

2 A sample of 400 fish is taken from a lake, tagged and released. Some time later, a second sample of 100 fish is taken and it is found that 5 of these have tags. What is the fish population estimate for the lake?

3 The ages of 16 students in a first-year university class are as follows:

17 17 17 18 18 18 18 18

18 18 19 19 19 20 21 44

Calculate the mean, median and range of this set of values, giving answers to 1 decimal place.

4 In the previous question, the oldest student represents an outlier. Recalculate the mean, median and range when this outlier is not included.

5 Below are the results of a survey of the hours of television watched by 25 Year 8 students over a weekend. Draw a histogram of the data.

Hours of TV	Number of students
0	1
1	5
2	7
3	7
4	3
5	2

6 Test results (%) for a Year 8 maths class are listed:

48 93 75 62 61 58 45 70 41 45

95 82 74 71 58 63 77 85 58 49

Starting with an interval of 40–49%, draw a histogram of the data.

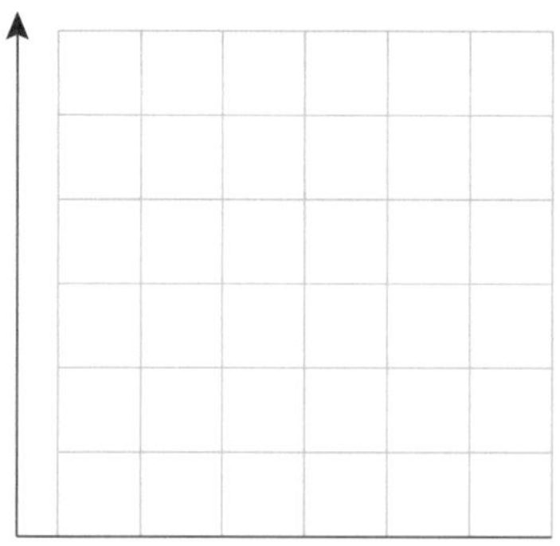

Practice 9A mark: /6

  ISBN 978 1 4886 1403 3

Pearson Mathematics 8 Homework Program

Statistics and probability

Skills 9B

Skills & Practice: Total marks /25

Name:

Class:

Teacher:

This side of this worksheet reviews number skills. The other side of this worksheet refers to *Pearson Mathematics 8* Chapter 9 'Statistics and probability' sections 9.4 and 9.5.

1 Complete the table below:

	8	-7	12	11	-9	4	-10	5	-6
− 6									

2 Complete the table below:

	-32	72	64	-88	-16	96	-80	24	-48
÷ 8									

3 Evaluate 20 406 ÷ 100.

4 Evaluate 2300 × 90.

5 What are the next two numbers in the sequence?

2, 2, 6, 30, 210, …

6 What is the lowest common multiple of 16 and 24?

7 Evaluate $-9 \times -(8 - 7) \times (6 - 5) \times -(4 - 3) \times 2$.

8 Evaluate $\frac{3}{4} \times \frac{2}{3} \div 1\frac{1}{3}$.

9 What is 0.992 299 rounded to 5 decimal places?

10 Simplify the ratio 56 : 16 : 44.

11 Evaluate 0.7 × 0.7.

12 Evaluate $3^2 \times 3^3 \div 3^4$.

13 Solve this equation.

$2(h + 3) = 2(2h + 1)$

14 Simplify $8gh + 4g - 3h + 2g + 2hg$.

15 Find the value of the angle w in this diagram.

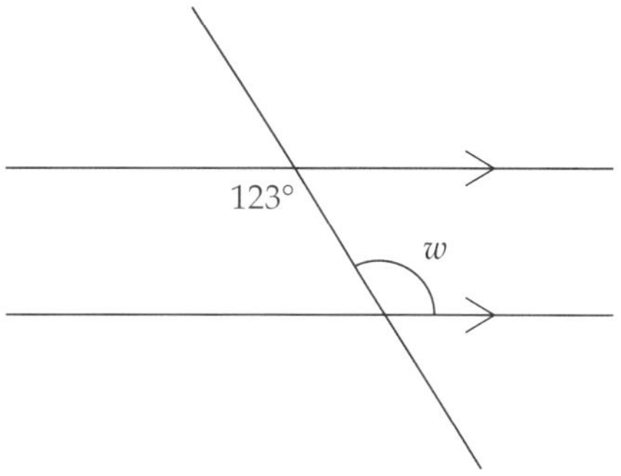

16 What is the class centre of a class interval of 40–49?

17 If a rectangle has an area of 24 cm^2 and a perimeter of 20 cm, what are its dimensions?

Skills 9B mark: /17

ISBN 978 1 4886 1403 3

Pearson Mathematics 8 Homework Program

Statistics and probability

Practice 9B

Show all your working

This side of this worksheet covers *Pearson Mathematics 8* Chapter 9 'Statistics and probability' sections 9.4 and 9.5.

For online help, go to your *Pearson Mathematics 8* eBook.

A group of 40 Year 8 students are surveyed to find the number of hours per week each student spends using electronic devices (smartphone, tablet, computer, TV etc.).

The table (at right) shows the number of hours spent in a particular week. Use the information in the table to answer the first four questions.

Hours	Frequency
0–<5	10
5–<10	18
10–<15	9
15–<20	2
20–<25	1

1 Calculate the mean number of hours spent in a week using electronic devices.

2 Find the median hours (class interval) spent in a week using electronic devices.

3 State the modal hours (class interval) spent in a week using electronic devices.

4 Identify any possible outliers.

Use the following information to answer the following four questions.

Nicole has 30 pens, of the following colours: 15 blue, 8 red, 4 black, 2 green and 1 purple.

5 If Nicole takes a pen at random, what is the probability that she takes a blue pen?

6 Nicole's friend Kelly has borrowed Nicole's purple pen. What is now the probability that Nicole takes a black pen if she takes a pen at random?

7 Kelly returns the purple pen. What is now the probability that Nicole takes a green pen or a red pen?

8 Nicole is given a 4-colour pen that can write in blue, red, black or green. She adds this to her 30 pens. What is now the probability that Nicole takes a pen that can write in blue?

Practice 9B mark: /8

  ISBN 978 1 4886 1403 3

Pearson Mathematics 8 Homework Program

Statistics and probability

Skills 9C

Skills & Practice: Total marks /27

Name:

Class:

Teacher:

This side of this worksheet reviews number skills. The other side of this worksheet refers to *Pearson Mathematics 8* Chapter 9 'Statistics and probability' sections 9.6 and 9.7.

1 Complete the table below:

	-5	7	-11	6	-9	4	10	-8	12
× -12									

2 Complete the table below:

	12	-36	30	-24	48	-54	-72	66	-60
÷ 6									

3 Evaluate 0.043×1000.

4 Evaluate $24\,900 \div 30$.

5 What are the next two numbers in the sequence?

2, -10, 50, -250, …

6 Express 72 as a product of its prime factors in index form.

7 Evaluate $-9 \times ((8 - 7) \times -6) + 5 \times -4$.

8 Evaluate $3\frac{2}{5} - 2\frac{1}{2}$.

9 Arrange these in descending order.

$1\frac{2}{5}$, 1.44, $\frac{9}{6}$, 1.404

10 If a car is travelling at an average speed of 50 km/h, how far will it travel in 2 hours?

11 Evaluate $0.06 \div 0.2$.

12 Evaluate 5×10^2.

13 Solve this equation.

$$\frac{2x}{3} - 1 = 5$$

14 If $x = 5$, find the value of $x(x + 1)$.

15 If the following points form a line when joined, what point is the x-intercept of the line?

(2, 2), (1, 1), (0, 0), (-1, -1)

16 Luke asked nine of his friends how many people live in each of their households. Their responses were: 2, 4, 3, 6, 4, 3, 3, 5, 4. What was the most common response?

17 A cube has a volume of 64 m^3. What is its side length?

Skills 9C mark: /17

ISBN 978 1 4886 1403 3

Pearson Mathematics 8 Homework Program

Statistics and probability

Practice 9C

Show all your working

This side of this worksheet covers *Pearson Mathematics 8* Chapter 9 'Statistics and probability' sections 9.6 and 9.7.

For online help, go to your *Pearson Mathematics 8* eBook.

1 What is the probability of rolling a number less than 5 on a standard six-sided die?

2 What is the probability of rolling a 7 on a standard six-sided die?

3 A ten-sided die has the numbers from 0 to 9 on its faces. What is the probability of rolling a number that is divisible by 4?

4 All the diamonds are removed from a standard pack of 52 playing cards. What is the probability of taking a heart from the altered pack of cards?

5 Amy changed one of the numbers on a standard six-sided die. Using the following probability statements for her changed die, find the number Amy changed and the number it was changed to.

- Pr(number less than 4) = $\frac{1}{3}$
- Pr(even number) = $\frac{2}{3}$
- Pr(factor of 6) = $\frac{1}{2}$
- Pr(number greater than 2) = $\frac{2}{3}$

In a Year 8 class, 24 students were asked if they wanted to play basketball or hockey. Their choices are shown in the Venn diagram at right. Use it to answer Questions 6–8.

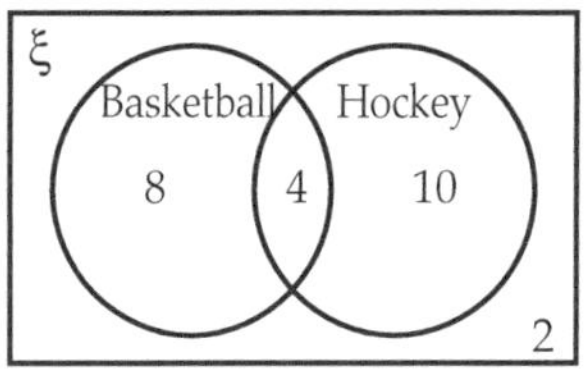

6 If a student is selected at random, what is the probability that they chose basketball only?

7 If a student is selected at random, what is the probability that they didn't choose basketball?

8 If a student is selected at random, what is the probability that they chose hockey or basketball?

9 A coin is tossed and a standard six-sided die is rolled. Use a table to list all the possible outcomes. From this find the probability of the coin showing tails.

10 Using your table from the previous question, find the probability of tossing heads and rolling a number greater than 4.

Practice 9C mark: /10

ISBN 978 1 4886 1403 3

Pearson Mathematics Homework Program 8

Answers

Chapter 1

Skills 1A

1

	-9	4	-7	12	-5	11	-3	8	-6
+ 6	-3	10	-1	18	1	17	3	14	0

2

	132	-44	99	-11	55	-110	33	-88	121
÷ -11	-12	4	-9	1	-5	10	-3	8	-11

3 190 000 **4** 128 **5** 162, 486, 1458 **6** 1, 2, 4, 8, 16, 32

7 -6 **8** $\frac{19}{16} = 1\frac{3}{16}$ **9** $7\frac{1}{4}$ **10** $110

11 8.3 **12** 121 **13** $\frac{x}{3} + 4 = 10$ **14** 23

15 210° **16** $\frac{1}{2}$ **17** 10 000 cm^2

Practice 1A

1 -4 **2** 8 **3** 0 **4** 19

5

7	-7	-6	4
-4	2	1	-1
0	-2	-3	3
-5	5	6	-8

6 negative, positive, negative, positive

7 -10 **8** -4

9 5 × -1 = -5
Ethan owes $5.

10 40

Skills 1B

1

	8	-3	12	6	-11	7	-4	-9	5
× -8	-64	24	-96	-48	88	-56	32	72	-40

2

	-54	36	-99	27	-108	81	72	-45	63
÷ 9	-6	4	-11	3	-12	9	8	-5	7

3 120 000 **4** 52 **5** 25, 12.5, 6.25 **6** 60

7 4 **8** 3 **9** 0.37 **10** 25% **11** 1.163

12 16 **13** $u = 0.9$ or $\frac{9}{10}$ **14** $17u + 7v$

15

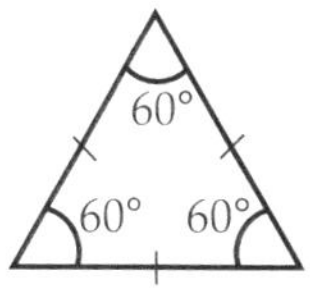

16 $\frac{1}{6}$ **17** 9 cm

Practice 1B

1 -8 **2** 10 **3** -4 **4** 10 **5** $1

6 3 **7** 2 **8** 3 **9** 10 **10** -2 °C

Skills 1C

1

	-3	4	7	-12	8	11	-9	10	-6
× -6	18	-24	-42	72	-48	-66	54	-60	36

2

	96	36	-108	60	144	-72	48	-84	132
÷ -12	-8	-3	9	-5	-12	6	-4	7	-11

3 5 600 000 **4** 91 **5** 12, 24, 48 **6** 97 **7** 4

8 $1\frac{1}{2}$ **9** $\frac{5}{3} < 1\frac{7}{9}$ **10** 60% **11** 0.8 **12** ±10

13 $x = 3$ **14** 11 **15** 30° **16** 10% **17** 135 cm^2

Practice 1C

1 3^5 **2** 5 × 5 × 5 × 5 **3** 2^{11} **4** $2^3 = 8$

5 $(-2)^2 = 4$ **6** 3 **7** -32 **8** negative

9 $(-3)^9$ **10** $2^5 = 32$, Ashley owes $32.

Skills 1D

1

	5	-7	11	-6	9	4	10	-8	-12
− 4	1	-11	7	-10	5	0	6	-12	-16

2

	-32	80	56	-72	40	-64	96	-48	16
÷ 8	-4	10	7	-9	5	-8	12	-6	2

3 267 **4** 119 200 **5** 35, 48, 63 **6** $2^2 \times 3 \times 5$

7 6 **8** 2 **9** $5\frac{1}{4} < \frac{85}{16}$ **10** $\frac{3}{10}$ **11** 7.2

12 5^4 **13** $5xy + 9x$ **14** 7 **15** 6

16 football **17** xy

Practice 1D

1 $2^3 \times 5^3$ **2** 1 **3** 5^{27} **4** $3^8 \times 2^{12}$ **5** $\frac{5^3}{7^3}$

6 $(3 \times 5)^4 = 3^4 \times 5^4$ **7** $5^2 \times 3^4$ **8** b^{12}

9 $x = 4$ **10** $3^3 \times 2^2$

ISBN 978 1 4886 1403 3

Pearson Mathematics Homework Program 8

Answers

Chapter 2

Skills 2A

1

	-5	10	9	-2	4	11	-6	8	-12
− 10	-15	0	-1	-12	-6	1	-16	-2	-22

2

	21	56	84	35	77	49	63	28	42
÷ 7	3	8	12	5	11	7	9	4	6

3 127 000 **4** 315 **5** 19, 22, 25 **6** yes **7** -1

8 $2\frac{1}{5}$ **9** $\frac{3}{4}$ **10** $70 **11** 1.91 **12** 36

13 $2x + 4 = 10$ **14** 29 **15** 60° **16** February

17 9000 seconds

Practice 2A

1 $\frac{1}{4}$, 0.3, $\frac{1}{3}$, $\frac{2}{5}$, $\frac{5}{9}$, 0.6 **2** 3 each with 16 left over.

3 2.625 **4** $\frac{9}{50}$ **5** recurring **6** irrational

7 $0.7\dot{2}$ **8** $\frac{14}{15}$ **9** -0.4 **10** $-\frac{1}{6}$

Skills 2B

1

	2	7	11	4	8	12	3	9	6
× 3	6	21	33	12	24	36	9	27	18

2

	90	30	60	110	10	120	70	40	100
÷ 10	9	3	6	11	1	12	7	4	10

3 28 **4** 7134 **5** 25.2, 25.0, 24.8 **6** 32 **7** -12

8 $\frac{17}{15} = 1\frac{2}{15}$ **9** $\frac{26}{72}$ **10** 75 kg **11** 0.95

12 64 **13** $3x - 6 = 9$ **14** 45 **15** 110°

16 basketball **17** 750 m

Practice 2B

1 50% **2** 70% **3** 25%

4 Various answers are possible. **5** 25% **6** 85%

7 37.5% **8** 36.2% **9** 125% **10** 60%

Skills 2C

1

	6	-12	3	9	-4	7	-2	8	-5
× -4	-24	48	-12	-36	16	-28	8	-32	20

2

	-66	36	-12	48	-72	24	-54	42	-30
÷ 6	-11	6	-2	8	-12	4	-9	7	-5

3 8 **4** 7101 **5** $1\frac{7}{8}$, 2, $2\frac{1}{8}$ **6** 24 **7** 3

8 $\frac{1}{2}$ **9** 5.40 **10** 6 students **11** 56.1

12 27 **13** $x = 18$ **14** $4h + 6$

15 acute-angled triangle **16** 0.6 **17** 38 cm

Practice 2C

1 $\frac{3}{4}$ **2** $\frac{7}{8}$ **3** 0.27 **4** 0.0025 **5** $\frac{13}{200}$

6 96% **7** 12.5% **8** 14.29%

9 Sarah 90%, Riley 92%. Riley got the better mark.

10 30%

Skills 2D

1

	-7	2	-11	4	-8	12	-3	9	-6
− 12	-19	-10	-23	-8	-20	0	-15	-3	-18

2

	32	96	-16	56	72	-48	64	88	-24
÷ 8	4	12	-2	7	9	-6	8	11	-3

3 420 **4** 25 416 **5** 9.9, 9, 8.1 **6** 59 **7** 10

8 $\frac{3}{4}$ **9** $1\frac{5}{6} > \frac{5}{3}$ **10** 75% **11** 2.4 **12** ±12

13 $b = 17$ **14** -6 **15** 45° **16** not likely

17 12 cm^2

Practice 2D

1 120 kg

2 Yes. 5% of 100 is 5, 20% of 5 is 1; 20% of 100 is 20, 5% of 20 is 1.

3 $480 **4** 10 **5** 30 **6** 10.62 seconds **7** $88

8 $59.50 **9** $45 **10** $1420

ISBN 978 1 4886 1403 3

Pearson Mathematics 8 Homework Program

Answers

Chapter 3

Skills 3A

1

	7	-2	5	-9	6	12	-3	-8	4
− 9	-2	-11	-4	-18	-3	3	-12	-17	-5

2

	-12	36	24	-72	66	-18	60	-120	6
÷ 6	-2	6	4	-12	11	-3	10	-20	1

3 2500 **4** 1346 **5** $4, 1, \frac{1}{4}$ **6** 64, 32, 16, 8, 4, 2, 1

7 -4 **8** $\frac{31}{36}$ **9** $\frac{17}{4} = 4\frac{1}{4}$ **10** 28 kg **11** 8.6

12 900 **13** $s = 3$ **14** 21 **15** 300°

16 likely or not likely **17** 2600 grams

Practice 3A

1 **a** equation **b** -3
c $-7c, 6d, -3ab, 6, 2c, b$ **d** a, b, c, d **e** 6

2 **a** $\frac{2w}{7}$ **b** $-2d^2k$ **3** $2t - 4$ **4** 16

5

x	5	10	15	30	60
y	2	3	4	7	13

6 -2 **7** -8 **8** 4 **9** 5 **10** 113.04

Skills 3B

1

	3	-4	7	12	-8	11	-9	10	-6
× 5	15	-20	35	60	-40	55	-45	50	-30

2

	33	-44	88	132	-55	121	-11	-110	66
÷ -11	-3	4	-8	-12	5	-11	1	10	-6

3 8 **4** 3250 **5** $6, 2, \frac{2}{3}$ **6** 36 **7** 2 **8** $\frac{1}{6}$

9 0.005 **10** 92% **11** 37.9 **12** 1 **13** $w = 0.5$

14 $4 + 9i + 6k$ **15** rectangle **16** $\frac{1}{10}$ **17** $6x$

Practice 3B

1 $3c, \underline{cd}, 5d, -\underline{5cd}, 2cd^2, \underline{3dc}$ **2** a **3** $4h + 6k$

4 $2 + 2x + 7y + 3xy$ **5** $13s + 6g$ **6** $12e$ **7** 2

8 $3g$ **9** $-12fg$ **10** $4m$

Skills 3C

1

	3	-4	7	-12	8	11	-9	-10	6
× 2	6	-8	14	-24	16	22	-18	-20	12

2

	-72	132	-96	60	144	-48	108	-36	84
÷ -12	6	-11	8	-5	-12	4	-9	3	-7

3 43 **4** 19 845 **5** 21, 2.1, 0.21 **6** 2, 3, 7

7 -48 **8** $1\frac{3}{5}$ **9** $1\frac{5}{16} < \frac{7}{4}$ **10** 90% **11** 0.45

12 ±20 **13** $x = 2$ **14** 14 **15** 108° **16** $\frac{2}{3}$

17 12 000 mm^2

Practice 3C

1 $5b - 30$ **2** $15a - 12$ **3** $6def + 2d^2f$

4 $8bc - 14b + 3bc + 9c + 10b = 11bc - 4b + 9c$

5 $2x(y - 3) = 2xy - 6x$ **6** $6r^2s^4$ **7** $2(3e - 7)$

8 $x(y + 4)$ **9** $5e(3 - 5f)$ **10** $(x + 1)(2 + y)$

Pearson Mathematics Homework Program 8

Answers

Chapter 4

Skills 4A

1

	-11	2	-7	4	8	-5	9	-6	12
− 11	-22	-9	-18	-7	-3	-16	-2	-17	1

2

	-120	22	12	-4	6	-200	20	-16	64
÷ 2	-60	11	6	-2	3	-100	10	-8	32

3 29 800 **4** 257 **5** 12.52, 12.55, 12.58 **6** no

7 6 **8** $1\frac{1}{4}$ **9** $\frac{10}{3} = 3\frac{1}{3}$ **10** $1200

11 0.778 **12** 4900 **13** $x = 2$ **14** 2 **15** 4

16 26 **17** 56 litres

Practice 4A

1 2:3 **2** 2:5 **3** $\frac{3}{5}$ **4** 2:3 **5** 12:1

6 1:4:3 **7** 5:1 **8** 1.2:1 **9** 2.5 **10** 78 cm

Skills 4B

1

	6	-9	4	-7	-12	2	-11	5	-8
+ 12	18	3	16	5	0	14	1	17	4

2

	21	-9	24	-18	33	-15	36	-27	6
÷ -3	-7	3	-8	6	-11	5	-12	9	-2

3 6000 **4** 956 **5** 768, 3072, 12 288 **6** 72

7 10 **8** $\frac{8}{9}$ **9** 2.2 **10** 40% **11** 64.45

12 32 **13** $x = 10$ **14** $0.4k + 3.4m$ **15** (3, 2)

16 bird **17** 14 cm

Practice 4B

1 $n = 15$ **2** $n = 2.5$ **3** $n = 2.5$ **4** 9 **5** 150 cm

6 1:50 **7** 60 m **8** no **9** 15 cm

10 1:500 000

Skills 4C

1

	9	-5	7	-2	12	-4	8	3	-6
× -3	-27	15	-21	6	-36	12	-24	-9	18

2

	-36	90	-72	108	81	-54	18	-45	27
÷ 9	-4	10	-8	12	9	-6	2	-5	3

3 352 000 **4** 769 **5** $7\frac{2}{3}$, 7, $6\frac{1}{3}$ **6** $2^2 \times 3^2$

7 -8 **8** $4\frac{13}{14}$ **9** $\frac{17}{5} > 3\frac{4}{15}$ **10** 88%

11 0.08 **12** ±50 **13** $x = 5$ **14** 0.06

15 248° **16** $\frac{5}{6}$ **17** 360.36 m^2

Practice 4C

1 12 **2** $24:$36 **3** 400 mL:1600 mL **4** 200

5 4 **6** 143 cents per litre **7** 50 km/h **8** 8 h

9 63 **10** 35 km

ISBN 978 1 4886 1403 3

Pearson Mathematics 8 Homework Program

Answers

Chapter 5

Skills 5A

1

	6	-12	7	3	-8	-4	9	-5	11
× 2	12	-24	14	6	-16	-8	18	-10	22

2

	-72	42	-30	54	48	-12	18	-66	36
÷ -6	12	-7	5	-9	-8	2	-3	11	-6

3 12.3 **4** 4920 **5** 17, 23, 30 **6** 1, 2, 5, 10

7 -36 **8** $2\frac{5}{24}$ **9** $\frac{13}{4} = 3\frac{1}{4}$ **10** 48 minutes

11 9.5 **12** 4^3 **13** $x = 2$ **14** 36 **15** 12

16 7 **17** 1 000 000 cm^3

Practice 5A

1 120 mm **2** 112 m **3** 1.5 cm **4** 132 m

5 11 cm **6** 3.142 **7** 39.27 cm **8** 65.35 cm

9 25.71 cm **10** 66.0 cm

Skills 5B

1

	-5	-8	-12	6	-9	3	-11	7	-4
+ 6	1	-2	-6	12	-3	9	-5	13	2

2

	12	-40	28	-80	48	-120	16	-24	32
÷ 4	3	-10	7	-20	12	-30	4	-6	8

3 9.8 **4** 61 320 **5** 47, 51, 54 **6** 27, 99, 9

7 -12 **8** $5\frac{1}{16}$ **9** 0.318 **10** 2% **11** 8.129

12 $2 \times 2 \times 2$ **13** $x = 2$ **14** $3h^2 + h$ **15** (-1, 3)

16 2 hours **17** 52 cm

Practice 5B

1 4 700 000 mm^2 **2** 84 cm^2 **3** 30 cm^2

4 108 cm^2 **5** 240 m^2 **6** 288 cm^2 **7** 50.27 cm^2

8 113.10 cm^2 **9** 3.1 m^2 **10** 125.66 cm^2

Skills 5C

1

	12	-6	9	-3	-11	-7	4	-8	5
× 9	108	-54	81	-27	-99	-63	36	-72	45

2

	-16	4	-18	8	22	-12	24	-20	6
÷ -2	8	-2	9	-4	-11	6	-12	10	-3

3 35.6 **4** 215 600 **5** 33, 45, 59 **6** 37

7 -12 **8** $\frac{5}{42}$ **9** 12.02, 12.12, 12.21, 21.12, 21.21

10 50% **11** 3 **12** 2^5 **13** $p = 5$ **14** 3

15 40° **16** TT, HT, TH, HH **17** 51 cm^2

Practice 5C

1 164.53 cm^2 **2** 896.64 cm^2 **3** 208 cm^2 **4** $8063

5 20 000 cm^3 **6** 1470 cm^3 **7** 20 cm^2 **8** 12.47 L

9 45 cm^3 **10** 1.25 L

Skills 5D

1

	9	-5	7	-11	4	6	-12	-3	8
− 8	1	-13	-1	-19	-4	-2	-20	-11	0

2

	-120	36	-12	24	-48	108	72	-132	60
÷ 12	-10	3	-1	2	-4	9	6	-11	5

3 0.405 **4** 28 840 **5** 1296, 2401, 4096 **6** $3^2 \times 5$

7 -1 **8** $\frac{11}{12}$ **9** $\frac{11}{3} > 3.6$ **10** 10:1 **11** 11

12 30 000 **13** $r = 4$ **14** ±4 **15** 9 **16** $\frac{2}{3}$

17 462 cm^3

Practice 5D

1 6 h 44 min **2** 1530 **3** 9:40 pm

4 11:30 am **5** 14 h 28 min

6 It is only 5 am in Perth. **7** 3:50 pm **8** 12:10 pm

Pearson Mathematics Homework Program 8

Answers

Chapter 6

Skills 6A

1

	5	-12	-9	6	-8	3	-11	-7	-4
+ 8	13	-4	-1	14	0	11	-3	1	4

2

	54	-18	81	-63	27	99	-9	-72	36
÷ -9	-6	2	-9	7	-3	-11	1	8	-4

3 6.11 **4** 164 100 **5** $\frac{5}{6}, \frac{6}{7}, \frac{7}{8}$ **6** 1, 3, 9

7 -12 **8** $\frac{11}{10}$ or $1\frac{1}{10}$ **9** $\frac{25}{2} = 12\frac{1}{2}$ **10** 4:5:2

11 51.04 **12** $36fgh$ **13** $x = 9$ **14** 10

15 yes **16** 6 km **17** 4 units

Practice 6A

1 age, height

2 Yes; as the age of the baby increases, so does its height.

3

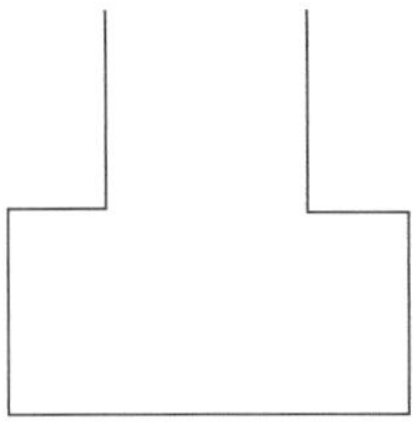

4

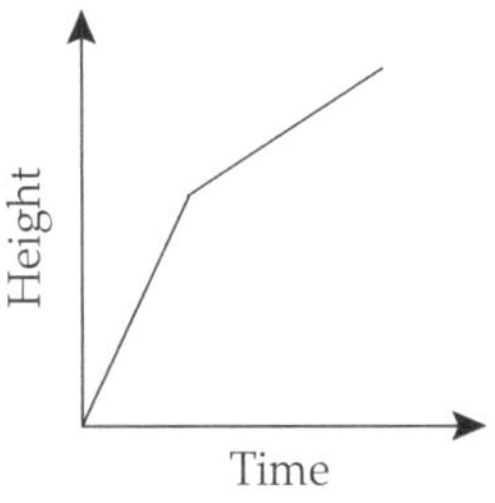

5 1300 m

6

x	-2	0	1	3
y	8	4	2	-2
(x, y)	(-2, 8)	(0, 4)	(1, 2)	(3, -2)

7

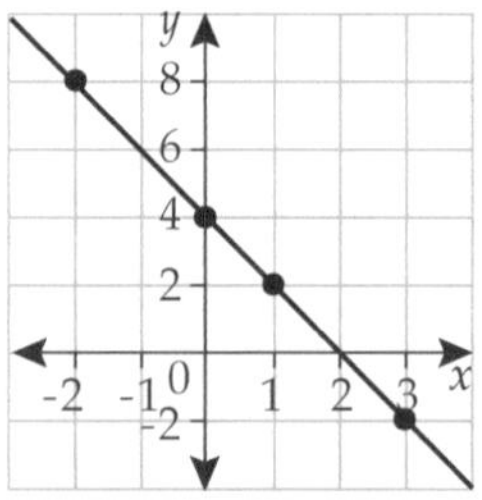

8 x-intercept (2, 0), y-intercept (0, 4)

9 $x = 3$ **10** negative

Skills 6B

1

	3	-9	6	-12	4	8	-11	-5	7
× -4	-12	36	-24	48	-16	-32	44	20	-28

2

	-30	5	-45	35	-15	40	-25	55	-20
÷ 5	-6	1	-9	7	-3	8	-5	11	-4

3 3.5 **4** 14 490 **5** $\frac{1}{32}, \frac{1}{64}, \frac{1}{128}$ **6** $2^2 \times 3^3$

7 2 **8** $\frac{9}{7}$ or $1\frac{2}{7}$ **9** 0.0016 **10** $\frac{17}{20}$ **11** 0.56

12 2 **13** $x = 25$ **14** $2g^2 + g + 5$ **15** 71°

16 $\frac{1}{26}$ **17** 19.54 cm

Practice 6B

1 $y = 2$ **2** $y = -2x + 2$ **3** -4

4 $y = x - 1$ **5** $y = x + 2$

6

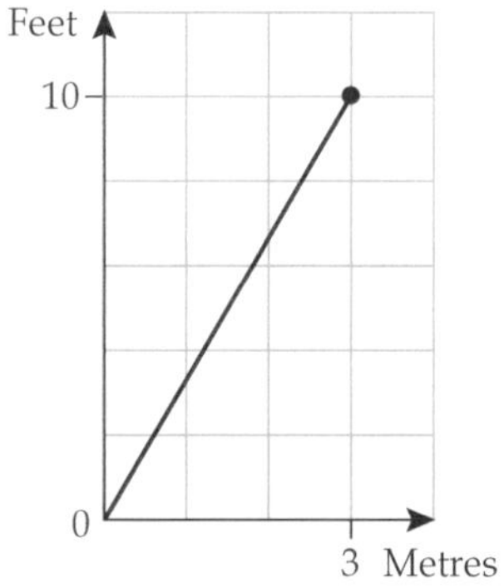

7 1.8 metres

8 3.3 feet

ISBN 978 1 4886 1403 3

Skills 6C

1

	6	-9	5	-12	7	-4	11	-3	8
$\times 5$	30	-45	25	-60	35	-20	55	-15	40

2

	-64	16	-48	32	-72	56	-24	96	-40
$\div$ -8	8	-2	6	-4	9	-7	3	-12	5

3 203 **4** 65 **5** 23, 23, 22 **6** 7 **7** 21

8 1 **9** $\frac{49}{3} = 16\frac{1}{3}$ **10** 5:7:10 **11** 1.11

12 $5n$ **13** $x = 9$ **14** 5 **15** trapezium

16 $\frac{4}{5}$ **17** 126 cm^2

Practice 6C

1

Length of wood (m)	0	1	2	3	4
Cost ($)	0	3	6	9	12

2

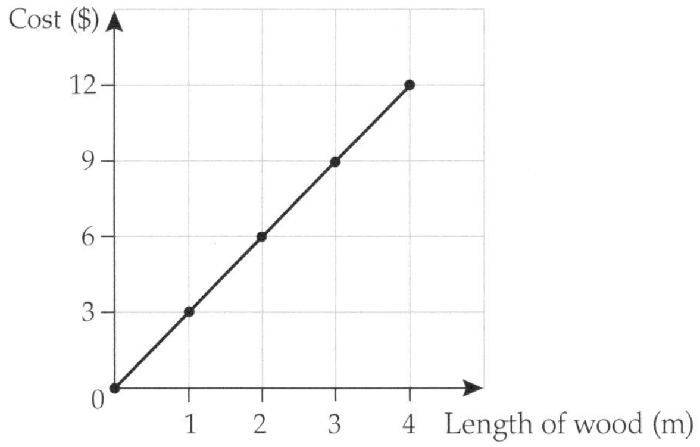

3 yes **4** $7.50 **5** 3.5 m **6** 5 m

7 Pronumerals may vary.
f = callout fee, h = hours of labour, r = hourly rate,
c = total cost: $c = rh + f$

8 yes

ISBN 978 1 4886 1403 3

Pearson Mathematics 8 Homework Program

Answers

Chapter 7

Skills 7A

1

	-5	7	11	-6	-9	4	-10	-8	12
− 7	-12	0	4	-13	-16	-3	-17	-15	5

2

	120	-36	12	-240	48	-108	72	-132	60
÷ -12	-10	3	-1	20	-4	9	-6	11	-5

3 259 **4** 3000 **5** 654 321, 7 654 321 **6** 12

7 -30 **8** $\frac{1}{2}$ **9** 0.1, $\frac{1}{9}$, $\frac{1}{8}$, 0.13 **10** 5:6

11 1.074 **12** $5 \times 5 \times 5 \times 5 \times 5 \times 5$ **13** $x = 17$

14 6 **15** 8 **16** 48 runs **17** 14 cm

Practice 7A

1 $2x + 3 = 18$ **2** $20 - b + 3 = 11$ **3** yes

4 $x = 12$ **5** $a = 4$ **6** $x = 18$ **7** $c = 12$

8 $x = 2$ **9** $n = -2$ **10** 6 years old

Skills 7B

1

	5	-7	11	-6	9	4	-10	8	-12
× 12	60	-84	132	-72	108	48	-120	96	-144

2

	-80	120	-100	30	10	-90	40	-60	110
÷ -10	8	-12	10	-3	-1	9	-4	6	-11

3 17 960 **4** 2000 **5** 123 454 321 **6** 168

7 -23 **8** 9 **9** 0.0037 **10** \$3 **11** 0.4

12 y **13** $x = 3$ **14** $jk + 3j$

15 (1, 3) should be moved to (2, 2) **16** $\frac{1}{2}$

17 114.27 cm^2

Practice 7B

1 $d = 27$ **2** $h = 14$ **3** $x = 8$ **4** $b = 5$ **5** $x = -5$

6 $r = 2$ **7** $x = 4$; the point of intersection is (4, 15)

8 $m = 1$ **9** $x = 2$ **10** $7x - 4 = 9x - 6, x = 1$

Skills 7C

1

	5	-11	7	-3	12	-9	4	-8	6
− 11	-6	-22	-4	-14	1	-20	-7	-19	-5

2

	21	-6	24	-12	36	18	-9	27	-15
÷ 3	7	-2	8	-4	12	6	-3	9	-5

3 658.8 **4** 30 **5** 100 001, 1 000 001 **6** $2 \times 3^2 \times 5$

7 -1 **8** $\frac{4}{15}$ **9** $\frac{17}{4} > 4.1$ **10** 3:2 **11** 4

12 $9cd^2$ **13** $x = 6$ **14** 24 **15** 115°

16 Friday **17** 120 m^3

Practice 7C

1 $x + 5 = 23$ **2** $x = 18$ chairs **3** $x + 2.5 = 5.3$

4 Salad roll $\$x = \$2.80$ **5** $2x + 2(x + 5) = 18$

6 $x = 2$ cm **7** $4b = 18$ **8** $b = 4.5$ cm

9 $x + (x + 16) = 130$ **10** $x = 57$ points

ISBN 978 1 4886 1403 3

Pearson Mathematics Homework Program 8

Answers

Chapter 8

Skills 8A

1

	-8	3	-6	11	-4	9	-5	12	-7
×3	-24	9	-18	33	-12	27	-15	36	-21

2

	88	-22	110	-44	121	-33	55	-132	77
÷ -11	-8	2	-10	4	-11	3	-5	12	-7

3 23 550 **4** 1660 **5** -32, 64, -128 **6** 90

7 16 **8** 6 **9** 0.403 **10** $\frac{21}{50}$ **11** 0.24

12 2 **13** $x = 8$ **14** ±5 **15** 65° **16** 7

17 75.6 m^3

Practice 8A

1 63° **2** 94° **3** e **4** 30°

5 110° (alternate angles are equal) **6** 35°

7 35° (angles add to 360°) **8** 18°

9 30 (vertically opposite angles are equal) **10** 32°

Skills 8B

1

	10	-2	12	7	-4	9	-11	6	-8
× -5	-50	10	-60	-35	20	-45	55	-30	40

2

	-12	40	-28	8	-48	12	16	-24	32
÷ -4	3	-10	7	-2	12	-3	-4	6	-8

3 0.05 **4** 17 990 **5** $\frac{1}{36}, \frac{1}{49}, \frac{1}{64}$ **6** 12

7 8 **8** $\frac{3}{4}$ **9** $\frac{21}{2} = 10\frac{1}{2}$ **10** 5:12:3

11 10.58 **12** $4u$ **13** $x = 18$ **14** 49 **15** 45°

16 5 **17** 78 cm^2

Practice 8B

1 40° **2** 120° **3** kite **4** 105° **5** true

6 40° (isosceles triangle, angles add to 180°)

7 70° (co-interior angles add to 180°)

8 60° (rhombus, angles add to 360°, opposite angles equal)

9 140° (symmetrical trapezium, alternate angles are equal)

10 40° (kite, symmetrical, angles add to 360°)

Skills 8C

1

	-8	5	-9	4	-7	3	-12	2	-6
+ 9	1	14	0	13	2	12	-3	11	3

2

	-56	21	63	-35	14	42	-84	28	-49
÷ 7	-8	3	9	-5	2	6	-12	4	-7

3 0.096 **4** 20 520 **5** 81, 243, 729 **6** 48

7 14 **8** $\frac{3}{8}$ **9** 0.081 **10** $\frac{13}{20}$ **11** 0.24

12 8 **13** $x = 6$ **14** $1.6p$ **15** 60° **16** $\frac{1}{2}$

17 22.0 cm

Practice 8C

1 **a** 3 units right, 1 unit up. **b**

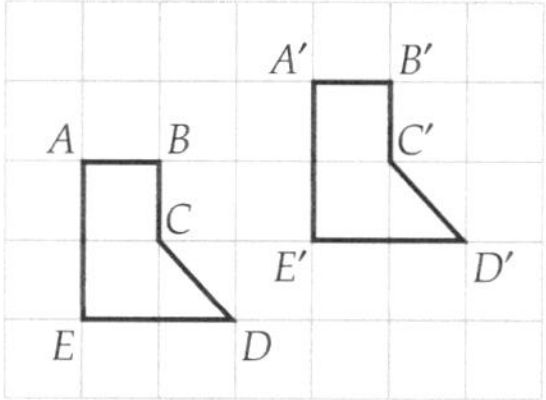

2 **a** $F \leftrightarrow V$
b $FG \leftrightarrow VT$
c $\angle AGF \leftrightarrow \angle ZTV$

3 $CDEFG \equiv HNMLK$

4 SSS

5 $YW = DC, \angle YWX = \angle DCE, WX = CE, \therefore \Delta YWX \equiv \Delta DCE$ (SAS)

6 $\Delta PTS \equiv \Delta RTQ, \Delta STR \equiv \Delta QTP, \Delta QPS \equiv \Delta SRQ,$
$\Delta PQR \equiv \Delta RSP$

7 $AB = CD, BC = DA, CA = AC, \therefore \Delta ABC \equiv \Delta CDA$ (SSS),
$\therefore \angle ABC = \angle CDA$

8 $LK = LM, KN = MN, NL$ is in both triangles,
$\therefore \Delta LKN \equiv \Delta LMN$ (SSS), $\therefore \angle LKN = \angle LMN, \therefore x = 100°$

ISBN 978 1 4886 1403 3

Pearson Mathematics 8 Homework Program

Answers

Chapter 9

Skills 9A

1

	5	-7	11	-6	9	-4	10	8	-12
× -11	-55	77	-121	66	-99	44	-110	-88	132

2

	-77	21	-35	7	140	-42	700	-49	280
÷ 7	-11	3	-5	1	20	-6	100	-7	40

3 0.5 **4** 86 **5** 600, 3600 **6** yes **7** -88

8 $5\frac{19}{20}$ **9** $\frac{25}{2} = 12\frac{1}{2}$ **10** $\frac{22}{25}$ **11** 3.62

12 $2.5q$ or $\frac{5q}{2}$ **13** $h = 1$ **14** ±7 **15** (0, 2)

16 $\frac{5}{13}$ **17** 516 cm^3

Practice 9A

1 All the customers will own at least one pet.

2 8000 fish

3 mean = 19.9, median = 18, range = 27

4 mean = 18.3, median = 18, range = 4

5

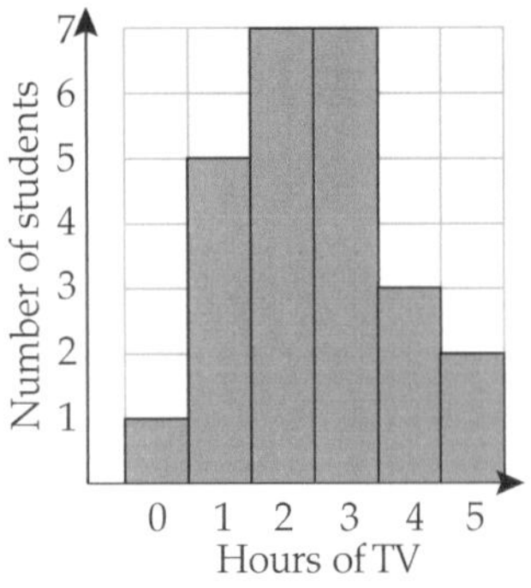

6

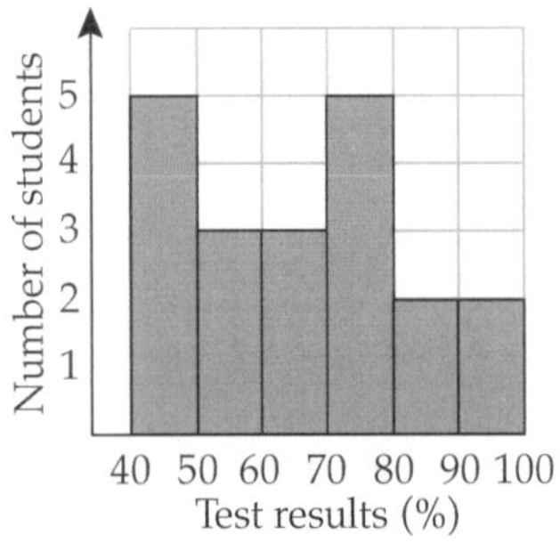

Skills 9B

1

	8	-7	12	11	-9	4	-10	5	-6
− 6	2	-13	6	5	-15	-2	-16	-1	-12

2

	-32	72	64	-88	-16	96	-80	24	-48
÷ 8	-4	9	8	-11	-2	12	-10	3	-6

3 204.06 **4** 207 000 **5** 1890, 20 790 **6** 48

7 -18 **8** $\frac{3}{8}$ **9** 0.992 30 **10** 14:4:11

11 0.49 **12** 3 **13** $h = 2$ **14** $10gh + 6g - 3h$

15 123° **16** 44.5 **17** 4 cm by 6 cm

Practice 9B

1 8.25 hours **2** 5–<10 **3** 5–<10

4 There don't appear to be any outliers.

5 $\frac{1}{2}$ **6** $\frac{4}{29}$ **7** $\frac{1}{3}$ **8** $\frac{16}{31}$

Skills 9C

1

	-5	7	-11	6	-9	4	10	-8	12
× -12	60	-84	132	-72	108	-48	-120	96	-144

2

	12	-36	30	-24	48	-54	-72	66	-60
÷ 6	2	-6	5	-4	8	-9	-12	11	-10

3 43 **4** 830 **5** 1250, -6250 **6** $2^3 \times 3^2$

7 34 **8** $\frac{9}{10}$ **9** $\frac{9}{6}$, 1.44, 1.404, $1\frac{2}{5}$

10 100 km **11** 0.3 **12** 500 **13** $x = 9$

14 30 **15** (0, 0) **16** 3 and 4 **17** 4 m

Practice 9C

1 $\frac{2}{3}$ **2** 0 **3** $\frac{1}{5}$ **4** $\frac{1}{3}$ **5** 3 was changed to 4

6 $\frac{1}{3}$ **7** $\frac{1}{2}$ **8** $\frac{11}{12}$ **9** $\frac{1}{2}$ **10** $\frac{1}{6}$

ISBN 978 1 4886 1403 3